FROM FATHER TO DADDY

REVAMPING OUR THINKING

AND

PERFECTING OUR PATH

DAVID A. WHITE

Indie Owl Press

Indie Owl Press

818 SW 3rd Ave #221-2455
Portland, OR 97204-2405

info@indieowlpress.com
IndieOwlPress.com

From Father to Daddy

www.DavidWhiteAuthor.com

First U.S. Edition, 2017

ISBN-10: 0-9990126-4-9
ISBN-13: 978-0-9990126-4-2
LCCN: 2017917753

Printed in the U.S.A.

Dedicated to fathers who take their role as daddy seriously,
and to the men who sincerely want to do better by their kids.

"It is easier to build strong children than to repair broken men."
— Frederick Douglass

CONTENTS

INTRODUCTION

When I had my first child at age 23, my father-in-law asked me at the time of birth how I felt. My response was one word: unprepared. I always looked forward to the actions required to conceive a child, but had not thoroughly thought out the inevitable life changes of becoming a father. I do not have a calamitous experience to share from my childhood; my dad has always been there as a working and loving man in our household. Interestingly, I cannot recall my father giving me a pep talk when I was becoming a father, but I figured his actions had laid out a blueprint to follow, and additional discussions were unsolicited by me. My inspiration for writing this book is not to tell a sad story, but to inspire and impress upon readers the importance of understanding the significance of the father role and how it is a unique and irreplaceable position in a family that should be supported and celebrated.

Children in households that are missing the father role often experience low self-esteem, and a persistent sense of unfulfilled desires. These households also combat challenges such as lower income, and hence decreased opportunities. I have a heart for two things in this world, the relationship between a boy and his father, and homeless individuals. Having an absent father or having a present, poor father in the home impacts male and female children differently. Both relationships are equally important. However, a boy having a nonproductive father will more likely become an ineffective father himself. Many of our societal-relational problems are the direct result of the absence of positive male figures in the home. It is time for the role of a father to be valued.

However, I am the first to admit that some households are better off without a father in the home. Period. Abuse and neglect are still substantial issues that fathers are inflicting on their children. These fathers are damaged goods who were mishandled as young men and did not know the correct way forward. Neglect can also be inflicted by a parent who just goes to work, comes home for dinner, and passes out with the help of an adult beverage in front of the television Monday through Friday.

Many men struggle with emotion dysregulation issues in that they do not know how to channel their stress appropriately or communicate constructively through these tense moments. Notice I said moments, because trouble does not last forever. Fathers are prideful when it comes to their role in the home, but it is okay not to have the answer or to ask for help in uncertain times without yielding to self-failure.

I remember watching the local news in San Diego back in 2008 during the home mortgage crisis. A man killed his whole family because he could no longer pay his mortgage and felt that he had failed as the provider and protector of the household. As a man, I know we feel the need to protect the family from all harm, which includes financial and physical hardship. Unfortunately, our families can also end up needing protection from us. That needs to end. In this book, I will discuss how the role of the father is more than protector. The father sets the stage for their child on how they may feel about themselves through adulthood.

Fathers do not have to be biologically connected to excel in the role as a father. Fatherhood is about sacrifice, love, and sacrificing some more. There are some patterns that we pick up from our father or mother, and those practices have not necessarily been updated or proven to be sound judgment. The stress level on fathers is tremendous, but the way we counter the stress does not always lead us to our best. The impact of a father can be good or evil. The number-one thing a kid does not want to do is disappoint their dad. Unfortunately, there have been fatherly roles in a church (priest) or sports teams (coach) that have manipulated and misused their influence. Adverse actions by men in our society have helped the shift of households substituting that role.

There are also some non-traditional families that have two women raising children together. This book is not to discount their efforts or methods. We all know that love and attention are what kids need, and anyone can provide those essentials. However, this book is to speak to all who have a father in the home and for men who have kids to support. The "traditional" model of a family, man, woman, and child, will always exist, but it is time to minimize the father's dysfunctions and maximize their value.

In the recent ESPN documentary "30 for 30: Brian and the Boz" it talked about Brian Bosworth having a flamboyant college career in the 80's in Oklahoma. Brian did some great things on the field, some questionable things off the field and on the sidelines. However, what stood out to me in this documentary was the strain between him and his father. Like many cases we see, hear, or read about, Brian was never enough for his father.

I understand the desire for your child to succeed, but most importantly to give their best effort. For the most competitive parents, those who aim for high achievements, we first want to know if our kid tried their hardest. Did our child give their best effort? In grade school on my progress reports, my teacher would often write a note saying, "Child's ability is not meeting effort." As parents, we're often not sure if the assignment or task is too hard or if the child is just not trying their best. I believe that Brian, like many kids, was giving an enormous amount of effort, and despite succeeding, his dad feared that simple praise would make his son relax in his efforts. Non-recognition may be a common thing among fathers when they do not want their kid to let up on the gas.

However, morale boosters are not just for the workplace; these things should first happen in the home. If my supervisor never said, "Hey, good job on the report or presentation," I would not be motivated to work harder or repeat that behavior. People want to be appreciated for a job well done. Yes, our kid's job is to do well, but our job as parents is to thank them or acknowledge them for meeting the expectation. Someone may say, "Well, maybe Bosworth's father's expectation was for him to be defensive player of the year in the National Football League, not a college champion or legend. I would say in school, we recognize every grade level of completion. We cannot celebrate high school diplomacy without sixth grade graduation.

Refusing to acknowledge progress does not only undervalue the child's successes but ultimately their self-esteem. The sad part about Brian's story is that he never got to enjoy his awards and achievements because it was never enough for his father. Often times a child's greatest honor is to hear his dad say, "You have made me proud." What children want most is to please their father then imitate them.

When my son David Jon was three years old I was walking from the carport to our condo, and slightly tripped, but I made it look cool. David Jon was walking behind me, and he repeated my action even though it had been an accident. I took notice, but I wanted to make sure I understood what was happening, so I did a jump kick and shouted out, "Whoa!" David Jon repeated that action as well, and that is when I noted that I better be careful because this boy is using me as a model.

Some fathers are exposing their kids to actions that are both good and bad but do not understand that their children are storing it all with a very high probability of repeating those behaviors. Parents are always guiding. We are life tour guides for our children with work shifts that never end. I know it can be a scary thought, but I love the fact that my children's eyes are continuously on me to lead them until they can lead themselves. My goal is for them to exceed my successes and avoid my mistakes. I LOVE BEING A DADDY.

My love runs deep for my children, and it gets tested. When I was 12 years old, I almost drowned at Newport Beach. Luckily, the waves calmed down enough for me to return to the shore. I told myself then that I would never go in the ocean again. I moved to San Diego, went to the beach for years, but never got in the water. In 2010, on a family trip to Hawaii, my son was four, and he wanted to get in the water. Well, I had a dilemma, but I could not afford for my son to get in the water without my supervision. After 15 plus years, I waded into the ocean, shelving my fear for the affection of my son. Countless fathers do not come out of their comfort zone and end up forfeiting time or meaningful memories with their kids.

I played the piano growing up; my dad was not a musician, but from time to time he would ask me if I could play a song by this or that artist and that built a connection between us. Children are looking for approval and attention, even if their past time activity is not the preference of their parents. Yes, there are some macho dads—Randy Savage—out there, who admittedly distance themselves from activities that are less masculine. This is a mistake in my opinion. What if single mothers who have to raise boys did not invest time or attention to their sons who want to play a sport, assuming that mothers are not sports fans. Thank God for moms likes Gloria James, the mother of LeBron James who raised him alone. Now, LeBron is not only a successful athlete and business person, but has excelled as a loving father. There are many triumphant stories of single mothers with positive outcomes in spite of disadvantaged circumstances.

When a child is abandoned, rejected, or missing a parent it determines if that child is burdened with a void or scar. When a parent is not around due to death or work, it may create a void. The situations when a parent leaves—a parent failing to form a relationship or an abusive parent losing interest or showing zero interest in a child—may leave a scar, and result in the child perpetuating the cycle of abandonment with their own kids. I am a firm believer, however, that emotional and physiological scars can be repaired. If my book assists in restoring even one relationship between a child and father, then it will all have been worth it.

I am not perfect, but I'm always striving to be a better me, which includes having self-awareness of my blind spots. Recognizing a blind spot causes a person to bury their pride and broaden their perspective. Being a father can be a prideful role, and it is natural for people not to listen to someone who they do not agree with most times. There are a wide range of possibilities for failure, it is not necessarily a singular event, especially when the Father title goes to any man who helps to conceive a child. As such, there is more involvement in earning the Daddy title. When my kids use the phrase daddy, it unconsciously makes me step up to meet their request. I like being the daddy. When my wife calls me daddy, it results in extra arousal in that moment. The title daddy comes through sacrifice, love, and leadership. In this book, I will address typical fatherly mistakes, ideologies, and highlight the role of a father. Constant improvements are necessary for leadership positions, and there is no greater charge than leading your children. Moving from father to daddy takes honesty, self-assessment, and a willingness to change.

FROM FATHER TO DADDY

Chapter 1

More Than a Protector

I recall a day when I was five-years-old riding my little red bike in our neighborhood. I had made it to the end of the street, which was a few blocks long, when a neighborhood dog got loose and began to chase me. I was scared and screaming. I went from peddling at 8 MPH to what felt like 18 MPH. The dog was on my tail the entire way, barking. No dog-owner in sight. As I approached my house, I screamed out, "Dad!" while swerving from the street to the sidewalk to the grass. As my bike hit the grass, my pace slowed, and I eventually fell over on my bike screaming and squirming. Still a yard from my house, my dad was running to the rescue with a baseball bat in hand. Just as the dog lunged to bite my leg, my dad was there to intervene, and hit the dog away. After that event, through my five-year-old eyes, I looked at my dad like he had a huge "S" on his chest.

From an early age, I had always viewed my dad as the protector because he was more physically intimidating, and obviously had a deeper voice and stronger presence than my mom. However, when she needs an ice-breaker for a presentation, my mom likes to share a story about me. It goes something like this...When I was a toddler, I was playing on the jungle gym at a park, and I made my way to the top of the apparatus. I was too scared to come down, though, thinking I would fall: I panicked and began to cry. My mom rushed over to me, climbed to the top, and brought me down. I said, "Mommy, I did not know that you can be a daddy." Yes, my youthful perspective could only see a male as the protector.

If a family is asleep at night and there is a strange noise or a window breaks in the kitchen, the expectation is that the man of the house responds to the commotion. These are natural instincts for the male role. However, if Daddy is out of town, or not around the mother is going to take on the role of safeguarding the home and children. There has to be some flexibility in the roles at home. When Mom is not around, Dad should be expected to prepare meals, make sure everyone is properly bathed, and support social activities. Just being the protector and provider of the home can be pleasurable and give men a sense of self-worth. However, the duties do not stop there. Society got it wrong when we started saying that raising children is a job. In the workplace, we have position descriptions (PD), and if a duty is not in our PD we generally won't engage in that task. Men are direct and task-oriented creatures, and we like to stay within our role and comfort zone. The history of the father was not always a multitask job, and specific responsibilities of the family were gender-based. Showing vulnerability and sensitivity can be challenging for fathers because it has not been a typical expectation.

Caring for children is not similar to having a job. As the parent, we are always on shift, and we are not trading time for money. The PD of a father is not just to protect; it has to be more open to ignoring gender specifics. Being a father is not work, it is a privilege to be blessed with the opportunity to raise and develop another human being that can positively contribute to society. You might be raising the child that develops cures for diseases, or becomes president of a successful company, or they may create new technology to advance our society. Sometimes we put limitations on what is possible for our child and that directly affects our children. It is sometimes difficult to see the greatness or the potential in others, especially if our own past is dimmed.

I understand we are living in a time where we are trying to erase gender roles and empower everyone as equal, which has its merits. However, I still choose to live and believe that men represent physical strength, and it would be silly to think that males are not the natural and intended physical protectors. Even in my casual day-to day interactions, I have watched male toddlers instinctively stand up for their mom without hesitation.

One of the most recent and disturbing news stories directly related to this topic involved a toddler named Jamil Baskerville, and poignantly illustrates the length to which a male child will go to be protective. Jamil lived in New Jersey, and at age two intervened in a violent argument between his mother and her 24-year-old boyfriend, Zachary Tricoche. The boyfriend allegedly punched the toddler in the chest, causing him to fall into the wall and hit his head. The toddler made it back to his feet, and then was ordered to square off like a cage fighter and put his hands up to fight. These orders allegedly came from the boyfriend who hit Jamil a second time, causing little Jamil to lose consciousness after a blow to the abdomen that lacerated his liver, resulting in internal bleeding and the two-year old's subsequent death. Trichoche is now on trial and charged with first-degree murder.

As a father, or even just a person who values humanity, I have irritated feelings about this entire incident. First, mom, you have to protect your children even if it costs your life. Mothers have to do a better job selecting who is fit to be around their children. Secondly, the apparent immediate thought is *what kind of person would challenge and physically strike a toddler?* Tricoche does not deserve to breathe another day, but looking at this incident in depth: Tricoche obviously has some psychological and emotional deficiencies. How did Tricoche get to the point where he decided to be the perpetrator rather than the protector? I know many men who, when put in intense and/or potentially violent situations, choose to leave. Leaving as an unsolved issue is better than violence or harm to innocent bystanders. Violence mostly occurs with parties who fail to communicate properly or effectively. People have to recognize what they're capable of during intense emotional situations, and remove themselves from the situation when necessary. Everyone is capable of snapping under pressure or a high degree of mental stress. However, it is never acceptable or excusable to violently harm a child under any circumstances. Tricoche lacked maturity, intelligence, and I am assuming a positive father influence to guide him correctly. Poor young Jamil lost his life because of his protective instinct, and having to live in a home with a man who did not possess qualities necessary to be an adequate leader, protector, or emotionally stable adult. There are many children in jeopardy of losing virtues of their life because they are in households with fathers who do not pour love, ambition, acceptance, and value into the young people they are raising. When a single mother decides to include a boyfriend in the home, by default the child perceives both adults as role models and protectors.

I have a son who lives primarily with his mother, and I am very interested in the man who will be part of my child's life, even if it's for a season, reason, or lifetime. As a mature father, I have to support my child's mother in finding a new love, and not allow my feelings toward her to cloud my judgment regarding the partner she chooses. My son's safety—physical and emotional—should be my primary and only concern. Going from two adults raising a child to potentially four, all grown-ups must be on the same page concerning unified methods and care for the child.

Protection does not start and stop at physical harm; emotional abuse can have long-term negative effects on a child as well. However, it can also be harmful to have a child around an adult with even just foul language and bad personal habits. There is a difference between bad habits and adult habits that can turn into bad habits for a child. Are we raising our kids to be just like us, bad habits and all? I do mask by adult habits and bad habits from my kids. Not by any means am I a mistake-free dad, but I do understand the power of exposure. Some certain medications and treatments are harmful to kids because of age limitations, or liver and kidney development. Exposing children to profanity, smoking, sexual content, cheating, and alcoholism is not conditioning them to "reality." When becoming a parent, it is healthy to do self-inventory or visit a counselor that can help discover childhood baggage that was problematic and capable of bleeding into future relationships. Every behavior or lesson our parents showed us might not have been the best method or way. As people, we do better as we know better.

The common issue we hear is "my parents did this to me, and I turned out okay."

Corporal punishment has always been a controversial topic in American households. Saying, my parent, spanked me when I was misbehaving as a child and that is why I now spank my child is not justifiable. The purpose of physical punishment for kids is to correct wrong behavior, and the physical pain is supposed to deter the child from repeating the bad behavior. Spanking being the only answer to problems with all kids is lazy parenting. Different strokes for different folks. Meaning, all children do not learn the same and they do not process correction the same way. I received spankings as a child but before the spanking, there was always a speech and understanding of what I had done wrong. Post-spanking, there was a speech, a hug, and kiss given by my parents to let me know they are going to love me through the mistakes but I must make better choices.

In some cultures, there is a common belief that I am spanking my child to protect them, so when they are unsupervised, they act appropriately. I remember when I was a young father and married to my first wife, she had a daughter named Dylan. I called Dylan the villain because when she was age two and three she was super ill-tempered and often getting into trouble. Dylan's mother and I both spanked her attempting to correct the behavior. I believe there is a time in a child's life where there is a power struggle, and the child does not comprehend who is in charge, and there needs to be some respect established within the parent-child relationship. One day, when Dylan was three years old, I heard her in her room yelling and pounding on something. As I entered her room she looked up at me, and I said, "Dylan, what are you doing?" She replied, "I am spanking my baby doll because she peed on herself." She was going bananas on the poor doll. I initially laughed, but as I took inventory of the situation I thought to myself, Dylan loves this doll, and she's beating the stitching off of her, *is this what she thinks is the only way?* Was Dylan repeating this behavior because this is what we had exposed her to?

Men, we are still viewed as the hammer in the household, and we are also responsible for the emotional development of our kids. I am mainly referring to emotional regulation, which is the ability to manage frustration and develop better impulses. As parents, if our first reaction is to flip and hit, what behaviors do we expect our children to acquire? There is a way to administer corporal punishment in an efficient manner while establishing love and control. Unfortunately, some households turn corporal punishment into a violent scene. Violence produces no resolution. Children have different learning styles and respond to various disciplinary methods. I have two boys: one needs to be physically directed to do something, and the other requires a firm conversation. I cannot parent them the same way because they are two different people. Assuming that all kids will respond to spankings is lazy thinking and parenting.

Ultimately, we want to motivate and encourage our children to do right according to the values that we have instilled. Just like adults are not driven by the same things, neither are children. One of the biggest things for parents to comprehend is that sometimes we have to protect our children from our past and the false blueprint that we inherited.

The one gift that many good parents wish they could give their children is a balanced self-esteem. Protecting your kids from suicidal thoughts or deep depression can be a blind, unpredictable task. Some children deal with this as a disease because of mental health, and others deal with this because of the lack of nurturing to their self-esteem. Dad's, we are more than a protector, we are preventers with maintenance characteristics, by habit. The top purchases by men are cars, electronics, and homes. After we acquire these products, what we do next is get tools to upkeep the look and value of the goods. As early as 16-years-old, after I got my first car, I purchased Armor-All for my wheels, glass cleaner for my windows, and polish to preserve my paint job. When a child is out of order, in disarray, or life is wearing down their thread, dad is supposed to intervene and protect the value of the child. Establishing self-esteem happens early in a child's life. When I got my new black Jeep in my 20's I was not flaunting off the jeep four years after driving it, I was parading it around immediately. Children form a self-concept or understanding of themselves at an early age, and it is the daddy's responsibility to instill those qualities in their child early.

I recall the story of former NFL star Terrell Owens and learning about his childhood and how it was identical to my own fathers' experience. Both Terrell's mother and my grandmother had a relationship with men who were already spoken for, and it resulted in Terrell's conception as well as my father's. My dad and Terrell had to grow up in the same neighborhood living in a different house than their father, and both had no knowledge that the man they saw around the neighborhood was their father. A man told Terrell at age 11, "You cannot like this other little girl in the neighborhood because that is your sister." That same man failed to tell Terrell that he was his father as well. My dad went to school with a girl that looked like him and had the same last name as him. He did not know that his classmate was his sister until later in life. Both Terrell and my father were rejected and left in the dark about who was supposed to be the leading man in their life.

The consequence of rejection for any child can last a lifetime, especially without proper healing. Terrell admits later in life that the impact of his dad failing to own him or be responsible for him caused him to develop an attention complex. Terrell's story is tragic because when he made it to one of the biggest accomplishments of his life in the NFL, scoring 153 touchdowns, all eyes were on him, yet Terrell never felt he received the attention a child deserves from his father. His dad, the protector, had overlooked Terrell for years. As such, and rightfully so, the TO persona was created, begging for the world to look at him because the man who was supposed to provide maintenance and attention had failed to. Terrell is like many men and women who have experienced rejection from a parent.

There is a necessary ingredient to providing a child with balance and wholeness. When daddy fails or when dad is absent it is like putting a cake in the oven after forgetting to add the eggs to the batter. Yes, there are substitutions for eggless cakes, but you may sacrifice the usual fluff or sweetness. The lack of a father's love, attention, presence, and support will disrupt the outcome of the child. When fathers intervene later in life, you almost have to go back to the very beginning when the batter was mixed. My dad and grandfather's relationship mended but was never restored to a degree that could have replaced what was lost. The impact on my father was that he became overly committed to my grandmother, most likely because, out of the two parents, she was the one who taught my dad the most about sacrifice and love. The amazing thing about my dad having an unsettling relationship with my grandfather was that it made him determined to be a better father to his kids. It is never too late to restore a relationship between parent and child; however, the parent must own their wrongdoing and start at the beginning of the disconnect. Protection as the father is just not enough, preventive measures and maintenance are just as crucial in upholding the value of our children.

CHAPTER 2

LOVING WITH YOUR HANDS

When a child comes out of their mother's womb, the father, when present, is generally rejoicing and overjoyed—anxious to get the first picture with the baby on mommy's chest. They take the baby home, and as the baby gets to about six-months-old dad is sleeping with the baby on his chest regularly. There are enough kisses and hugs to go around for everyone. Before you know it, the kids are asking not to be treated like a baby in front of their friends. The child's innocence wears down and they start to do things to disappoint the parents, particularly dad. Many men, including myself, like to be the enforcer of the household rules. There is a difficult balance between being the enforcer and coddling the child. Men want to raise little men but the problem is that the father's definition of a man is flawed. I have witnessed some fathers excel in the home as a provider, a cook, a coach, a teacher, and protector. A well-rounded father knows how to love with their hands.

I always thought, what if my child was deaf or lost their hearing? Would I show affection through my body language as I do through my speech? People retain a low percentage of what they read and see; however, we retain 100 percent of what we feel. Even when that feeling is wrong or hurtful it is retained more accurately. For people who are physically or sexually abused, it's the feeling that gives them the urge to shower and wash off—not just the unwanted touching but the experience. An unwelcome touch makes people flinch or their skin crawl. The power of touch is undervalued. There are critical moments in life when words cannot solve or bring resolution to the problem. Only a touch, a hug, or a kiss on the forehead can remedy the issues in that moment.

From a very early age, we make touch a norm in our culture as a way to connect or feel approval. When I was growing up, an adult would ask a kid for a high-five to break the ice or say good job. Now, the kids are doing fist and chest bumps. A young athlete makes a good play on the field and the coach pats him or her on the butt while echoing good job. As a college student it is normal to greet your buddy with a hug and handshake. When a person is sad or crying, the expected reaction is to rub their back as a sign of comfort. Touching is a part of human expression.

Expressing care, love, and security to our children must be done through physical touch. Healthy affection will then become a norm in the household. If I am lying back watching TV, I want my kids to be able to come sit next to me and lay their head on my shoulder. Many professional nurses have testified to the power of touch and holding an ill patient's hand. Fathers, we need to get back to loving with our hands and words, while not feeling like you are softening up yourself. However, as far as I'm concerned, if I have to appear soft for the benefit of my children, then call me Charmin tissue because my kids emotional needs come before my image, social status, and thoughts of others.

As a father, one of my biggest fears is making sure that I am creating more good memories. The memories we deposit with our kids are eventually going to imprint on them, unconsciously or voluntarily. I was telling my mother just the other day that I had heard a line on the television show *Modern Family* years ago: "A father's number-one job is just to show up." I agree to an extent, and interpreted this as meaning that far too often father's may be absent from various events during their children's impressionable years. The reasons for this are varied no doubt. Some justifiable and some inexcusable; however, I think the main job of a parent, particularly a father, is to create positive memories that their offspring can reflect on for esteem or later emulation. For example, I have taken my oldest son to places like Hawaii and the White House in Washington, D.C. to help create positive memories. Memories of gifts are great, but the recollection of having given your time and attention is better.

Not being able to recall if your parents kissed you as a child is a disservice to the relationship of child and parent. The purpose of parenting is to steer. When we ride a bike, or drive a car, steering is the key component in not crashing. You can be riding fast or slow, but how and where you turn determines whether you arrive at your destination safely. When my five-year-old and I are out walking in public at Disneyland, I am either steering with my voice or turning his body in the direction I want him to go. No matter how old your children get, while they are still young, the physical steering may decrease but the father's voice should always be active as a friendly form of navigation. The fathers voice and demeanor can sometimes be intimidating to the child, but a way to decrease that barrier is to correct with your hands not just your voice. Playing youth football, if I made a mistake, sometimes the coach would show me in the playbook what route or option I should have taken. If the coach really wanted to impress the message but with a supportive tone he would take me under his arm to explain the mistake. Both ways do work, but the latter let me know that the coach really wanted me to be successful.

Potty training is a stressful and difficult task to complete for both the parent in the child. I had the responsibility of potty-training both of my boys. It was not easy but I did not make the same mistake with my youngest son that I made with the eldest. With my eldest son, David, I was physically aggressive in the sense that I dragged him out of bed after wetting himself and made him stare at the toilet. There were times I spanked him for not using the toilet, to the point where he feared wetting himself and woke up in the middle of the night at an exaggerated rate. Sometimes resulting in urinating only a few drops in the toilet. With my younger son, Isaiah, I did more of the teaching with my arm around his shoulder style. I did more exercises with him, seeing daddy properly peeing in the toilet and sometimes urinating in the same toilet at the same time, so Isaiah viewed potty-training as fun, playful, and a positive experience. Since then I have used the coaching-arm as my main tool with both my kids to show them I want them to be successful. Yes, they also know my discipline hand, but so far, I have nurtured better results with my coaching arm. Fathers, we can use our hands to build, maintain, or to destroy, lets choose building and maintenance.

I recently watched a documentary on Steven Gleason. I was already familiar with his accomplishment as an NFL player for the New Orleans Saints. I knew after his retirement he was diagnosed with the Amyotrophic Lateral Sclerosis disease. ALS is a neurodegenerative disease that affects the brain and spinal cord. Not only are the nerve cells in the brain thrown off course, the bodies muscles get weak, lacking nutrition to the point where a person with this disease can no longer breathe on their own. There are many positive takeaways from the Gleason documentary, but for the sake of this book I want to highlight the parts that are applicable to this chapter. First, I do not get in the habit of calling public figures heroes of mine; however, Mr. and Mrs. Gleason are heroes in my world. After being diagnosed with ALS, they both found out they were having a child. Part of the purpose for his documentary was to leave video messages while he was able to express himself in a normal state for his son to review later in life. As his son grows as a young toddler, Gleason's body is deteriorating, but the love for his son remains steadfast. By the time Gleason's son is two-years-old, he wishes he could pick him up and spin him around in the air. Gleason is unable to display any action with his hand but is more deserving to do so than majority of the able fathers in the world. It is extremely difficult to maintain a relationship with anyone when you have physical limitations. And it is despicable when someone misuses their powers or takes for granted the little blessings that life gives us. Watching Gleason transporting his toddler on his wheel chair, pleading for his wife to bring him close for a kiss, or adoring his son while his friends play with him on his behalf is heart-wrenching for me as a father. I am a fan of fathers who want to do right and try their best to positively impact their kids. Having the ability to love with your hands and choosing not to is an incorrect path as a father. Dads, we are super heroes to our kids by default. Your kids will look up to you as the example, the noble one, and the hero, until they have another man they can compare you to. This is not always a bad thing if you like honesty and do not mind knowing your real value as a father and a man. Either way, a father can be his children's hero by default until your child gets into the early adolescent years. If you are a good man, you can maintain the hero status through personal deeds and actions. There are some men who are 40-years-old and still view their dad as a hero. Obviously, that father has done continuous maintenance to maintain the relationship between him and his children.

As a parent, it is important to know the difference between pressure and expectation. These terms impact our children in different ways. My parents had expectations for me to conduct myself a certain way in and outside of the home. My parents expected me to try my best and apply the knowledge of cause and effect in everything I did, whether in academics or athletic activities. One year, my dad coached me in basketball—I was in the sixth or seventh grade. Yeah, I'm sure he got frustrated with me when I missed open lay-ups, but I never felt the pressure to perform at a certain level or else I would have to deal with his wrath later. My dad is no slouch and neither am I, though; we are both competitive in everything we do, especially card games and racquetball. But our competitions have always been derived from a healthy, motivating source. Yes, we do hear stories of parents being demanding of their kids and it paying off. The truth is there is not a one-size-fits-all formula; you have to know your kids and learn how to motivate them to bring out the best. Being the father of the house is, in many ways, equivalent to being an office manager. Kids need to be loved, but their personalities need to be managed. Lazy parenting is when you treat all of your kids the same. Pulling the right strings to get your child to meet your expectation is rewarding, but it's not fair to just say, "Do it because I said so," especially if you are known for saying contradicting things. Sometimes Dad's may push their kids because they see talent or laziness. It is a pet peeve of mine to be on a highway and see a Corvette driving slowly in the fast lane. I say, "Why does this person have a fast car with torque, but are letting it under-perform relative to the car's abilities?" I know that Corvettes can fly on the road so I want to see it fly. Dads often know what their kids are capable of, and sometimes we just want to see them perform at the level we know they're able. The intentions are not wrong, but sometimes the methods for motivation need to be re-evaluated and adjusted.

Being affectionate correlates with parents helping to create their kids love-language. We are creatures of habit and patterns. If a person grows up in an atmosphere where there is not enough physical touch or pats on the back, the child may think that lack of affection or withholding affection is normal, or that physical touch is just strange. When we think of Gary

Chapman's different love languages, we always associate this with romantic relationships. There are kids who prefer material gifts. There are Dads who would rather forfeit money than their time. Quality time is as important as affection. Whether parents can afford to give elaborate gifts or not, quality time with their children is priceless. And words of affirmation during quality time are vital to a kid's self-esteem and self-confidence. Acts of helpful service can even include projects like washing your kid's car without them asking. Growing up, I always heard girls say, "I want to find a man like my daddy." The man that this woman ends up with needs to know how her father showed love because that is what she is conditioned to expecting and responding to. This goes for the amount of physical affection she's accustomed to experiencing as well. Loving with your hands is healthy because there is healing in the hands. I'm not speaking from a spiritual perspective precisely, but people respond to gentle touch as they do to a gentle voice. As fathers, we need to remember that we have power in our hands to form and to destruct. The effects of which last a lifetime, influencing many types of relationships in our children's lives.

A man should use his hands for skill, power, and usefulness. If a man is a carpenter or holds an occupation that requires him to repair anything, his hands are a necessary tool. It is difficult to fix anything without the use of his hands. To demonstrate strength, the hands are required. I have known some men who use their hands to intimidate or to motivate. I have given firmer than usual handshakes as a sign that I am not a push over or desire to be challenged. When a person arm wrestles, an old trick is to get the hand and wrist bent early on the opponent to gain the advantage. There are kids who flinch out of fear around their dad when he so much as raises a hand. A father can demonstrate power but it should never be with the intent to harm the kids or their mother. That power should be manifested in a way intended to pick them up and carry them when they are physically or emotionally weak or tired, or to defend them in times of danger. A father's skilled hands are best utilized when shared with their children. If your background is as an electrician, plumber, carpenter, mechanic, etc. Share those traits with your kids so they can become better and more useful contributors to their generation whilst garnering a stronger sense of self-worth and purpose that they will in turn share with their own children. As violence begets violence, kindness, skill, and patience begets kindness, skill, and patience.

CHAPTER 3

BUILDING TO BE BETTER

One of my favorite movies while growing up was *The Five Heartbeats*. At the time I saw it I was a young musician, and this was the perfect movie to capture a piano player's attention. In the film, the lead singer is beginning to gain success and believe in his talents. After an excellent performance, he is heading home, and the people in the city are cheering him on and offering encouraging words. However, as he arrives home he runs into his parents, and his father says to him, "You ain't going to be shit because I ain't shit." As a teenager, I thought that was a funny line in the movie. Even though it was rude of his father to diminish or squash his dreams, the lead singer was really disappointed to hear his father not support him, and hear that he expects failure for his own son's future. Looking back on that movie with a more mature perspective, I am now disgusted by the father's reaction to his son's talent. I cannot justify a parent crushing a child's dream. As a father, are we competing and defeating, or inspiring and admiring? A parent's job is to help their children believe in their dreams even if they seem out of reach. A common saying is if you work hard you can achieve anything.

As parents, we have to believe in our children beyond our imagination or belief. It is common as we get older to operate within a realistic and safe zone. Meaning, the decisions we make, and the choices we steer our children to make, often fall under the umbrella of a realistic goal and a safe option. As parents, we are looking to shield our kids from failure and broken dreams, but failure is a part of success. There was a funny commercial with retired professional basketball players Latrell Sprewell and David Robinson, and the quote was: "Success is failure that hasn't happened yet." This quote is coming from somewhat of a pessimistic perspective, so I prefer to reverse it when applying it to goals and dreams. Failure is success that has not happened yet. At times of failure, everyone has an opportunity to build grit, determination, preservation, and anticipation toward an improved outcome the next time around. My eldest son loves to quit an activity or game if he is stinking it up. This same boy can be good at a particular game or activity, but once someone better joins the game, he may fold and quit. Quitting is not acceptable. I have always coached him to take the beating and learn from the loss so he can improve.

As a young piano player in the church back in the late 90's, people would sing or request songs that were sung in the 70's before I was even born. I had a choice not to play and let them sing without music or I could call up an elder musician to play the tune and hinder my growth. However, I choose to endure the humiliation and pick through the song, affecting the flow of the song for my learning improvement. Knowing that I am failing or reducing the quality of something motivates me more. I do not like being the weakest link on a team, and if I am, I will disguise it and contribute in another way. Challenging myself to improve is a good trait to have and a good trait to pass along to my kids. It is not automatic that my son will have the same determination as me.

I am passionate about competition and turning my weaknesses into strength. If I fail a class, I want to take it again because I think I can learn the concepts or material next time around. It's hard to develop passion in a child, either they care sincerely for that thing or not. However, we can help our children to form healthy interests. As parents, we often want our kids to develop the same passions that we have toward a topic or belief. We get unsettled with our children and wonder why they do not think or care about a particular interest as we do. I know my eldest son gets easily discouraged, so my goal is to get him comfortable and accepting of the process to improve. I regularly show him where he's at, where he was, and where he could go. Accepting improvement is the thinking that I guide my son to be content with instead of worrying about the outcome. When it was time for my son to ride his bike without the training wheels, accepting improvement was the key to helping him overcome his fears and chase success.

Pursuing growth can affect a person's success rate and make them passionate about improving instead of winning or being the best. My eldest son, David Jonny—what I call him, was nervous about falling off his bike and getting hurt at age five. I said, "David Jonny, I am proud already because you do not have training wheels on anymore. And you have Daddy to help balance you on the bike while riding for now." I continued to say to David Jonny, "If you pedal through your fears and maintain calm steering, you will be alright. You will only fall once you stop pedaling, and probably crash if you stop steering."

As the days passed I got my son to ride longer with less of my assistance, and I would continually remind him where he was, how far he'd come, and where he could go. David Jonny got excited over his improvement and, fairly quickly, began making goals for himself. He would say, "Dad, give me a push-start and I am going to ride to the end of the street instead of just to the mailbox." For his safety, I would still jog right beside him. Fear of failure leads kids to quit, but the trick is getting your child to fall in love with the middle part which is the process. This method can be applied almost in any arena when trying to teach and guide developing children.

Growing up, I loved video games, and today my kids love to play video games. The lessons that video games teach us are not often acknowledged in their simplest form. I remember playing Mario Brothers, or Sonic the Hedgehog. When I lost on one level, yes, I would get upset, but never wanted to quit the game altogether. Like the video game, everything is about passing one level at a time. Our job as the parent is to ride beside to make sure our children are steering properly, or to provide tips to help our kids progress to the next level.

My father made sure for me—a young man who started a family early—to monitor my credit and maintain a stable income. My dad's position was to ensure I would avoid as many pitfalls as possible. A quiet parent, watching their kid ride through life without input, love, and guidance is not building to be better. There is no gratification in telling your child, "See, I told you so." There comes a time when your child is responsible for their path, but we need to establish a relationship that inspires them to want us in the role of the driving instructor riding in the passenger seat. To build a better relationship with their children, the parent needs to be within reasonable reach.

Advancing the lineage should be in the forethoughts of every man. Passing down a legacy to our children is what parents must aim for when creating a family. Yes, from a superficial view, it is always great when mom or dad leaves behind wealth. But what about knowledge? The family business? The principles and pride that the family name is honored to uphold? Sometimes there is nothing of value to pass on, but you can always pass on hope and a message to propel positive change within your family. There needs to be a message in the bloodline that is passed on throughout the generation. A message of progression, determination, and confidence. The late great professional boxer, Olympian, and activist, Muhammad Ali passed down his boxing skills to his Daughter Laila, and not only did she become a professional female Boxing Champion but Laila and her other siblings followed in their father's humanitarian footsteps as well. Bill Gates, a well-known business Mogul and philanthropist who made billions of dollars by leading Microsoft to industry and world success, credits his fathers' influence and positive example for his growth and development. Gates' dad was an attorney and man of integrity who passed noble attributes to his son. Both examples not only exemplified a strong work ethic but also showed a charitable heart for humanity. Building to be better is also about setting children up to launch from their parents' shoulders. Ben Stiller, son of actor and comedian, Jerry Stiller, often credits his success to his father for paving a well-lit path for his own success as a comedian.

Children inadvertently pick up on talents that their

parents expose them to, and in some cases the child genetically inherited a skill or trait that comes naturally. My dad is a compassionate man and has a big heart for people in need. Growing up, my dad talked my mom into sheltering multiple people when they needed a helping hand for a season. As an adult, I have always felt empathy for homeless people, and a lot of it has to do with witnessing those acts of compassion by my father. My mother is a well-educated woman who is a writer and has a natural gift for writing and performing uplifting poetry. During the first 33 years of my life I had only written for educational purposes or music lyrics. However, in the span of just seven months during 2017 I wrote three different books. Did I finally stumble upon my natural ability or was it the exposure of my mother? I recall being 12-years-old and going with my dad to his friend's house to visit. My dad's friend invited us to his backyard for a game of pool. I remember thinking to myself that my dad does not play pool. Boys do not like seeing their father lose in anything and fathers do not like losing in front of their kids. I watched my dad shoot pool like a novice, and surprisingly make 8 out of 9 shots. His friend and I were both amazed. After the pool game, my dad and I left laughing in victory, and this was the day I realized that my father is competitive at everything, but also willing to put his neck out and rise to the occasion when it benefits the enjoyment of others.

When I was in the tenth-grade, instead of hanging with

the "cool" kids or talking to girls, I started to watch my Asian American classmates play ping-pong. Many of my classmates thought ping-pong was a nerdy game, and when I became intrigued with the sport, those same classmates laughed at me. However, I started to learn the game, and after a few months I became competitive in pong-ping and even inspired other ethnicities to join the sport at school. We began to set up tournaments, and I would do well, but there were still others who were better than me. One day after school, my cousin and I were talking about ping-pong at my house and my father overheard. My dad said that my cousin and I could not beat him. I said, "You don't even play ping-pong." He replied, saying he used to play back in the 70's. We all ran out to the sports store to purchase a table and balls. For the rest of the afternoon, my dad took turns beating the fun out of my cousin and me on the ping-pong table. For the next several weeks, my dad and I would play or, rather, my dad continued to beat me. Meanwhile, while studying his form and strategy, I was learning and developing.

My father did not withhold his secret to success, and he was quick to share it with me after beating me dozens of times. What I noticed is that he plays mainly with his backhand with the paddle covering everything across his chest and rarely opens up for a slam. However, his secret was to make the opponent sabotage themselves as he maintains consistent and steady returns. My dad had a boring style, (like the San Antonio

Spurs Championship teams) and it would bait me into a kill shot, which is a low percentage shot. As a young man, I was into flash and style. Once I learned the patience of the game and developed multiple serving styles I became the champion of the house. I have discovered in my short life that patience is the key to success most of the time. While waiting patiently for an opportunity, a person must be preparing for the moment. A good parent is equipping their child for that moment of opportunity to seize success.

Some countries have a culture of teaching soccer or football, and the expectation is for these particular people to be better at it than everyone else. Yes, you can improve a skill in an individual who may not have the natural ability to be good at that particular thing. But more important than building the skill, as leaders of our home, we must build hope and confidence in our kids. Everyone needs hope and confidence at some point in their life, especially when approaching something new. Most successful adults who have a brand or a company that is leading their industry needs a team of people who are confident in their mission. The phrase "fake it until you make it" is not a misleading statement. It's hard to always believe in everything you attempt. Our children may not have the cognitive sense or wisdom to know about dusting themselves off when they fall on the ground. Hope and confidence are free and are often the leading driver to get people to succeed. People have accomplished things because other people believed in them more than they believed in themselves. Yes, a perfect world is when both parents and children believe in the outcome.

My hope is that a significant takeaway from this chapter will be an increased drive to instill hope and confidence in one's children. As the parent, we cannot always use our experiences to determine how we are going to manage our kids. For example, many people think that if I was able to accomplish this without support than the next person should be able to as well by just encouraging themselves. This statement can be partially true because self-confidence is a driver to victory as well. However, it is best to include our experiences and build our kids up with confidence because it increases the probability of their success. It's also important to do this with no regard for our personal path. We are not testing our child's limits and abilities, we are coaching and developing those areas that are lacking but have the potential for greatness.

In college, the official course title is "Child Development." Not child testing or child ruling! When you develop something, there are always phases to go through to reach completion, and completion is not just when they turn 18-years-old. Different phases call for different tools and approaches. A good dad should never stop the praise and communicating their belief system just because the child becomes a young adult. We need to support our children through every phase of their life and doing so is what defines a strong family. Support and a voice of hope should be a repetitive cycle in a healthy family. My intention for this book is not to define the perfect parent because there is no such thing. However, a healthy parental relationship can be pursued, cultivated, and achieved.

My competitive side is always looking to be a champion because we all like celebrating achievements. The ingredients to becoming a champion dad are footing and foresight. Having a good sense of balance and setting your feet in the proper direction while shifting the body weight is critical in all competitive sports. The competition of life is about approaching every situation with the most knowledge possible and knowing when to walk away from a dire situation. Having a good sense of what is necessary for the future or predicting what will happen, is the definition of foresight. My favorite athletes in the last 15 years have exceptional foresight, mental agility, and good footwork. Serena & Venus Williams, Kobe Bryant, Peyton Manning, Lebron James, Tom Brady, Aaron Rodgers, and Marshall Faulk. These athletes are all Champions and share similar attributes. These characteristics make a champion. We see athletes and judge them by how physically fit or "built" they are. Even though soccer star Cristiano Ronaldo is fit, it's the lower body strength that helps these athletes to finish the game strong. Footwork symbolizes balance, strength, and taking the correct path. As fathers, our goal is to provide balance, strength, and the right path for our household and children. One of the biggest things to balance as an athlete or parent is pressure to fulfill your expected responsibilities and block out distractions that can be detrimental to the completion of the task at hand. A champion athlete has mental toughness to maintain focus as they progress toward the goal, not just athletic ability. Mental toughness is the capacity to obtain success in a high-pressure environment with internal and external distractions and adversaries trying to sway your focus. Someone who is mentally tough keeps their eyes on the prize at all cost.

Building to be better requires us to teaching our kids how to block out unnecessary noise and distractions. We live in a time where cyber bullies can impact our children's self-esteem. Our children still deal with peer pressure that is consistently present more than ever. As the parent, we must have foresight when it comes to the children our kids befriend. As mature adults, we can often see indications for which of our kids' friends may be a bad influence or lack sufficient direction to prevent from leading our own children astray.

My dad became friends with my friends and friends of my brother's friends. I recall play wrestling with my friends against my dad even up to my high school years on numerous occasions. It was part of my dad's design that he would build a supplemental relationship with my buddies. When parents see a friend they do not approve of the first thing that comes to mind is for that friend to be removed immediately from their kid's friend circle. The method of immediate removal without discussion or minimum explanation will lead the child to a rebellious state. My dad connected with my friends for many reasons. Most importantly, some of my friends did not have a male influence as a positive example. The second reason was to form a mutual trust and respect for one another. Lastly, it was so that my friends would have a better understanding of my Dad's expectation for us as young men.

As a parent, if I know that my child's friends have 25% or more influence on their choices and decision-making, I want to use those friendships to my advantage. Thinking ahead and knocking down potential road blocks makes a champion dad. Turning a weakness into a strength is what players do in their private practice. Finding private time with our kids to correct and uplift is vital in the development process of building our children. Knowing if your kids respond to open or private criticism is going to help the approach and the recipient of the advice. Like I said before, just because I can endure public criticism does not equate to my children being able to perform under those same conditions. Each kid is different, the methods and approach may change, but the intentions and purpose never alter.

Is it possible to instill too much confidence in your child? Humility is an admirable trait in any person, but so is hunger. Recently in sports news, there was a father named LaVar Ball, who has a son starring on the basketball team at UCLA. He is also the father of two other high school prep stars. UCLA is a popular basketball program and his son Lonzo Ball is excelling on the court and destined for the National Basketball Association. Mr. Ball, the father, has made some bold predictions and assumptions regarding his son Lonzo. On national media outlets, he is on record stating that his son who is 19 years of age is better than Stephen Curry who is 28 and an NBA champion and two-time Most Valuable Player recipient. Many may have issues with the statement because his son's skills are unproven at the professional level, and he's discounting the achievements and efforts of Mr. Curry. It is never good to minimize someone else's achievements to boost your own; it is best to let your work stand alone. LaVar Ball is so invested and involved with his boys and pushing for their success that people have accused him of trying to live through his child vicariously and is too anxious to share the spotlight.

That said, it's important to remember that everyone is an expert on raising someone else's kids. People are naturally victims of implicit personality theory where their self-biases come into play with limited information on a person other than brief interactions and mere personality samplings. When people see a vocal parent pumping up their kid's abilities their biases of assuming arrogance, high-pressure parenting, and "meal-ticket" label are at the forefront of their minds. Because we want our biases to be correct, we look to justify or initial assessments of the situation or person. Every move that LaVar Ball makes, people will be looking to confirm their idea of him being a domineering or arrogant father who is taking the fun out of the game for his kids. When Mr. Ball does something that is opposite of what people expect of him, they discount those efforts. Society wants parent to be involved with their kid's activities but arrogance and humbleness can both be subjective terms. Mr. Ball's methods may not be the preferred choice, but it's difficult to make the determination that his intentions and heart are fraudulent or crooked.

Mr. Ball may just be creating a buzz, so scouts, sponsorships, and the public will take notice. So far, he has succeeded in bringing attention to his boys, especially the UCLA standout. LaVar played prep and college ball, but Lonzo has already surpassed his father's success on the court. One of the biggest concerns about LaVar Ball's outlandish approach is when he criticizes other student athletes he makes his children more susceptible to unsolicited criticism from the public. It is a selfish act to write checks that your kids have to cash. The positive side of this story is that their father is supportive, and from a competitive standpoint he believes that he has prepared his son for the basketball stardom that is the inevitable outcome. And in doing so he has geared his son up to handle playing under high expectations. When your child has natural abilities and stands 6' foot 8" inches, pushing them in a sport is the least a competitive father can do. Is there harm involved? Yes, if the father only cares about his basketball abilities and the child feels that's their parent's sole interest in them. There is also harm if the father's antics jeopardize future opportunities because the image of the family is undesirable to future teams or big brand sponsors. In this case, I prefer to assume that this father is going to love his boys whether they swim or sink. But the most important concern is how the children feel about the antics, predictions, and unsolicited attention. How do the kids feel concerning pressure to perform at a certain level? Does what Ball is doing fall under the umbrella of building to be better? The answer to all of these questions is subjective. The parent of these boys should know the depth of their character and what is a healthy amount of pressure. Also, parents do set the bar for their kids, not parenting authors or their neighbor.

What is the difference between saying my child is going to be a pediatrician or a school teacher? At the core, one profession may require a higher level of education and more schooling. Is it bad to shoot your kids for the stars? Just because the career of a professional basketball player is scarce with a small entry window does not make a person or parent foolish for making that the bar. Perhaps LaVar Ball's bar growing up as a kid was just to get a basketball scholarship, and that is all he was prepared to accomplish. So yes, building to be better is raising the bar and the standard. Everyone has the right to say where they want to set their bar. The only thing parents have to ask is if this is a bar that is healthy for their child and does our child know that we are going to love them even if they fall short? Perfect love intercedes for your kids when they fall short of a goal or standard set by the parents, child, or both.

Building to be better requires breaking apart the man in the mirror. Michael Jackson recorded a song about talking to the man in the mirror. Fathers, we have to do self-evaluation often to make sure that what we learned during our own experience maturing into adults is healthy for our children and makes sense for their needs and goals. Every step of the way, exploring what changes need to take place and using those challenges or questionable life decisions to benefit our kids. I have to teach my kids love first, then marriage, then a baby. It's also hard living under a different roof than the kids you love because there was a lack of love or commitment before creating the child, or it was eventually lost between the parents. I have experienced divorce, and sometimes you cannot always avoid divorce, but there is something beneficial that I can tell my kids about how not to repeat that action or at least ways to avoid divorce. Sharing those scars, wounds, and experiences that you see in the mirror with your kids will help them become better people. "A chip off the old block" is not good if that block is too flawed from the beginning.

Chapter 4

ADMIT MISTAKES

I am a person who takes pride in doing things correctly and efficiently. When I make a mistake, it bothers me because I consider myself to be detail-oriented while operating with a high level of common sense. When you are the leader of a project or group, it is unacceptable to your team when you seem lost or disseminate wrong information. I am easily annoyed by people who talk a lot so they can appear to be intelligent no matter what the topic may be. I am not one of those people, and I do not care for those type of individuals. If I have no useful information to add to the subject, I observe and listen. Fathers and leaders of the household sometimes get trapped in the mindset that they should always know the way and have the answer because we are the head of the home. Truthfully, I hate admitting that I made the wrong turn in the car. I would blame Siri or GPS before I'd admit why there was a delay in my arrival. I like to believe that my attention to detail is always up to par and that I do not make simple mistakes. Nevertheless, the truth is everyone is fallible—not just in their actions but our thinking as well.

In my early years of parenting, I made some mistakes that I was able to catch before causing additional damage. I always wondered what the main ingredient was for getting your child to succeed and work hard at a craft. We often hear stories of successful people and how hard their parents were on them, which is why they are now successful. I remember watching stories about the Jackson Five and taking away from that film lessons of hard work and discipline, wondering if physical discipline was the key to getting the best out of a kid. In other success stories I heard people say they could not eat dinner, or go to sleep until they got their routine perfect. Deprivation of some kind has been a tool used for years to get people to give their best performance. Sometimes, in an ignorant state, parents use force to get the desired outcome from their child.

My oldest son David Jonny was five when he showed an interest in playing the piano like me. I thought it was a good idea to start him off with the scales in C Major with the proper fingering. The next step would be to learn "Mary Had a Little Lamb" because it is easy and catchy. David Jonny kept making a mistake on the song, and it was starting to frustrate me because I thought this was a simple tune, and he just wasn't focusing. After ten minutes had passed, he was still making the same mistake, so I started to thump his hand every time he messed up. The more David Jonny screwed up the harder I would flick him. I noticed the mood change and all of a sudden he was more scared to get the note wrong than excited about getting it right. The piano is something I am passionate about, and I thought this was going to be a special night where I was passing my skill down to my son. Instead, I found myself upset because he was not catching on at a pace I felt was reasonable. It did not take long for tears to run down David Jonny's five-year-old face as he pleaded with me to stop the lesson. He said, "Daddy I don't want to learn the piano anymore, can we please stop?" I immediately stormed out of the room upset because he quit. All of a sudden, a feeling of shame and embarrassment overcame me. I lost my cool. I turned a precious moment into a pressured moment. I quickly examined myself right then and told myself: I am the one with the issue because I lack patience. I called David Jonny in the room with me, and he was still shaken up. I grabbed him and told him, "Daddy was wrong and I'm sorry." I had no right to flick your hand when you made an error nor did I make that experience fun. I began to cry because I was embarrassed and didn't know that I could lose control like that with my innocent, young son who was trying his best. I asked him for forgiveness, which he gave but we did not return to the piano. What is silly is that I have facilitated numerous piano lessons with kids and adults ranging from different levels of ability. Yes, as the piano teacher I was paid to have patience, but I assumed that just because the student was my child the learning curve would reduce. I constantly have to remind myself that my kids are not me, measuring them on their separate scale is a must, and some things may require more nurturing because it is not as natural for our children as it was for us.

Two things happen when you can admit to your kids or others that you made a bad call. First, it builds credibility with your children or the people you lead when you own up to your mistake. In most cases when a person has to show their flaws there is some humility attached to that uncovering. Secondly, saying sorry shows the people we lead that this is how you apologize and own up to your mistakes. The parent sometimes forgets to show their kids how to say sorry and how to forgive. There is going to come a day in all of our lives when we are going to need forgiveness, and we will owe someone an apology. I want to influence my kids to be well-rounded and understand how to handle themselves in favorable and unfavorable positions. No one likes a person who does not own up to their mistake or bad calls. Real leadership takes the blame even when it is a shared deed. In 2014, the Seattle Seahawks made a bad call in passing the ball at the goal line during the Super Bowl on the final drive, instead of running the ball, causing them to lose the biggest game of the season. Coach Pete Carroll stood in front of the media and accepted the loss, admitting the mistake. Similarly, Coach John Calipari said after the 2017 NCAA tournament that he should have called a timeout immediately after Malik Monk's game-tying 3-pointer with nine seconds left in Kentucky's 75-73 South Region final loss to North Carolina. My recommendation is for fathers or leaders of the household to review their decisions; sometimes a timeout is necessary to make sure you make the best call for your house.

When I was only around eight years old, my parents went on a trip to Hawaii, and my siblings and I were left in the care of a family friend. My brother and I, ages ten and eight respectively, got into a fight. Fighting was natural at that age for us boys. Mr. Smith, our interim guardian and retired military serviceman, thought we needed more discipline in response to our altercation. Mr. Smith spanked both of us with a vacuum cleaner cord. It brought my brother and me closer together, only because Mr. Smith instantly became the household enemy. It was not until Mr. Smith moved away, which was immediately after my parents returned, that we told my dad what had happened. My dad apologized, admitting that he had made a mistake leaving us in the care of that family. I'm not saying that family as a whole was a terrible family; other than the vacuum cord incident, I enjoyed spending time with the Smith kids. Even though my parents felt like they had vetted this family as quality people they were not familiar with their discipline style. Even years later, right up until my adulthood, my dad has apologized and admitted that mistake. I can appreciate that because it was an unforeseen mistake at the time. As parents, we make calls and later find out that it was not the best call, but how do we rectify that error? My dad was not upset about his misbehaving boys being disciplined, he was upset about the manner and method Mr. Smith had used. Children need discipline but for the right intentions, in a controlled setting, and suitable for the issue and child.

Maybe I punished my son because I was frustrated with his effort, or maybe it's a cultural norm. Even traditions and standard, culturally-accepted actions need to be analyzed, including corporal punishment. Children who receive spankings repeatedly do not necessarily cause less trouble or decrease their misconduct. However, at the time, I thought that kids who are disciplined with corporal punishment end up with a greater level of respect for their parents and their elders. Spankings have more of an impact on parental reverence with somewhat of an impact on keeping the child out of trouble. I have not discovered any research to support this theory more recent than Edward Thorndike's study regarding the "Law of Effect." However, substituting corporal punishment for prescription pills for your child is not favorable in my opinion. There are many effective forms of discipline; I am not a fan of spankings being the sole solution. As parents we have to be open to different methods that are perceived fair by the child and are developmentally and temperamentally appropriate. Respect and honor for your guardian does go a long way and is vital to the character-development of a person.

Beyond that, the honor that a child has for their parent's stretches beyond their adolescent years. In my experience growing up I knew which kids received spankings and the ones who did not. My friends who did not get chastised were combative and aggressive toward their parents by the 6th grade. However, spankings are not the only way to keep structure and boundaries between parents and the children. If a parent is whaling away at their child who is weaker and fragile in every way possible, they are misguided in thinking that leaving marks is an effective method for correcting wrong behavior. There are not too many parents willing to admit that maybe the way they punished their children is not the best and only way. Yes, I hear people say, "Spankings worked for me, and I turned out fine." But as parents, we should be aiming for the best solutions to correct our child's actions and not just settle for traditional methods but innovative ways to redirect their behavior. If I am programming my son that corporal punishment is the way to correct his behavior, what is the teacher at school supposed to use when he is off task? Spanking cannot be the only measure my kid responds to, and this is why parenting takes hard work and proper planning. When you plan to have a child, there needs to be a plan to handle that child in different phases and stages.

It is best to ask for help if you are having an issue with the child that you as the parent are having a hard time handling. People do not like to ask for help, especially in a room crowded with people or with a subject that they should already know. From high school to adult certification courses, people are apprehensive or too prideful to ask for help. Parenting is not a topic that anyone has the answer key for, though, and it is wrong to say it is *my child*, so I can do whatever I want with them. As long as whatever you want is in the child's best interest, most will not object. Exposing kids to adult issues, however, and things that are grown-up in nature is a mistake. Sometimes it takes people years to admit their mistakes even though it has been evident for a long time that it was a wrong choice. It is foolish for an individual to say, "I should have been a better steward of my credit and finances," now that their FICO score is 430. When a person's FICO score reaches 580, they should have admitted that mistake and made the necessary adjustments then. Another delayed but typical reaction is when a parent communicates to their kid when they are 19 years old, or a young adult, that maybe they should not have exposed that child to this or that particular behavior— *afte*r it is evident that it has negatively impacted the child. Most childhood damage does not occur overnight, but results from a series of unfortunate and unwise events.

I believe in taking off the hero suit and showing your

children the scars, bruises, and wounds that we as parents have endured along our journey. Sometimes as parents we wait too long to show our kids our imperfections. Building credibility with your child starts in the early stages. The good thing about a judgment-free zone is there is liberty for the truth to be shared. My goal, like most parents, is for my kids always to be forthcoming, even if the information shared is disappointing to me. My kids must know that I am on their side even after foolish mistakes, but as the parent and seasoned individual, my household culture needs to embrace those moments. My goal is not always to be the best friend or cool dad, but my children are an extension of me, and they need to feel supported, loved, corrected, and guided. Superheroes are emotionally numb to things when they are zipped up in their suit and only focused on the mission. Superheroes, generally, do not fall in love with civilians until they are out of costume and integrated back into everyday society. I try to relate to my kids in the present stage they are at in life and not always come from the authoritative or predictable platform, but have the sympathy for what they are going through because most likely I have been there before. It is especially challenging for parents at times because we can predict the outcome for our children if they choose to do this or that; however, the skill as parents comes from encouraging the right path and loving our kids back when they fall off that trail. Patience, as the parent, should be discussed more because some of our youngsters need more time in the oven than others.

One of the natural things that we tend to do is justifying our mistakes and poor decisions. A man is speeding in his car and is pulled over by the highway patrolman after nearly causing an accident. The officer tells the man that he is getting a ticket for driving 15 mph above the legal speed limit and reckless driving where he almost caused an accident. The man replies and says, "I was only speeding because I am late to work." We think that because our end goal is in the right place, we should not be penalized for the path in getting to that end result. People from troubled and low socioeconomic status areas may steal from the local food markets for the purpose of getting food for their family to eat, which is an essential need for all people, and hunger should matter to all. However, when the security guard catches the person in the act, saying, "I'm just trying to feed my family," does not justify the wrongdoing in the eyes of the law. Many people justify cheating on an exam, cutting in line, or downloading illegal music or movies because "everyone else is doing it." Does wrong become right when a majority is doing wrong? One phrase that I dislike that many parents use as a crutch is "I am doing the best that I can, with what I have to work with." Yes, I can understand and sympathize with that statement, but it does not get you out of jail for free. Doing the best you can may be having leftovers and spreading it out over three or fours days into different dishes to feed the family. Doing your best can be when you only have 15 minutes to spare, and you have to make dinner before leaving for the night shift so the family settles for cereal that night. However, as fathers and mothers, we cannot tell our kids we are doing the best we know how as a way to excuse our mistakes. When you are deficient at your place of employment, you do not say I'm doing the best that I know how. If you are deficient, you ask for more training or say you will improve in this area of weakness. Pleasing our kids should be more important than pleasing the employer. If a deficiency becomes exposed in our decision making or child rearing, we need to seek training from more knowledgeable parents or admit to our kids that we will improve and try to progress.

I also have an issue with any parent who is not transparent with their children. Transparency brings honesty in the relationship between child and parent. Yes, kids are watching us when we are happy, sad, hurt, or embarrassed, and we need to show the best way to deal with those issues even when we do not handle it right the first time. Does your kid know how to redeem a wrong action or mistake? Teaching in the home should never cease because there are lessons to learn in the home. Parenting is not directing your child in the day-to-day activities. I want my kids to do things on purpose and know why they are doing it that way. Kids have to understand the household plan at some point. However, some things are not for children's eyes or ears. Once again, we have to be mindful of what we are exposing our kids to even if they are big or seem "mature" for their age. Saying offensive things to your spouse or partner in the presence of the children is unproductive and damaging to the household. Unintentionally, it puts the child in an uncomfortable spot if this behavior is new to them. Our current society is immune to divorce and desensitized to adult confrontation and language. As the parents, we set the limits of what our child should be exposed to not societal standards. Do we ever say sorry for cursing at the dinner table in front of our kids anymore? Do we feel sorry for exhibiting road rage when our child is in their car seat repeating the gestures and language that we are giving to the other drivers?

The most harmful forms of damage often happen when one parent demeans or abuses the other parent in front of the children. Destroying the other parents' reputation happens in two ways. First, a parent can be harsh to the other parent in front of everyone. Second, the parent can bash the other parent in secret to the children or child. It is a mistake to steer a child in a negative direction where the child has ill feelings for the other parent because the adults do not get along. Separating feelings, and redirecting anger and disappointment takes a mature person who is putting the child's needs above their own. There are thousands of stories where a mother and father has fallen out of love and become enemies, but the child suffers because the adults cannot separate their feelings which denies the kid the rights to a fair non-polluted relationship with their mother or father. It is okay to run away from abuse and withhold the child from the abusive parent. It is not okay to keep a child away because the adult relationship ran its course or you think the other parent is immature. It sickens me when a mother makes the decision for the child and father that it's best they do not communicate or know the other parents' whereabouts just like it sickens me when a father neglects their responsibility of emotionally, socially, and financially providing. Sometimes an immature father who develops late is better than no father at all.

I recently heard a great story involving gospel singing legend John P. Kee. Kee has been composing and performing gospel music since the late 80's and is renowned among gospel music and Christian music circles. He has many awards with recognition coming from all across America. He is also the father of nine children. I had an encounter with Pastor Kee many years ago when he did a concert in San Diego. I was new to the city at the time and only 18-years-old. I arrived to the concert two hours early expecting to stand in line. However, I did not know that San Diego is inconsistent in supporting gospel music artists. When I arrived, they we completing the sound check, and they were short on a few instruments. I was eager to help in any way that I could, having grown up listening to this man's music. I let his band borrow my Keyboard and our church's new drum cymbals. He was shocked that I was so willing to help and I was surprised that he was thanking me so much. He even thanked me during the concert for having a helpful heart, and wrote me out a three-thousand-dollar check, just for borrowing my equipment for four hours, stating that he was giving me the check because of my generosity and attitude toward him. Pastor Kee's demonstration was also useful in showing the congregation that being nice in doing good deeds out of the kindness of your heart can result in a return for the person when they least expect it, like sowing a seed and reaping later. On that night I met Pastor Kee's son, Chris, who was his new drummer at the time, and I always thought that it would be cool to be the musician for your father's band.

In 2017 on YouTube, there was a clip titled "John P Key apologized to son for accusing him of stealing equipment from the Fat house studio." In this clip, John provides the background of the story, which took place over eight years ago, and involved some keyboards and drum machines that were missing from his studio called the Fat House. I know John P. Kee is a busy artist who tours every year, so equipment likely passes through a lot of hands and sometimes, as the CEO or overseer of the band, things can go missing unnoticed. However, Pastor Kee accused his son, Chris, of removing the equipment, possibly for Chris's personal benefit. Pastor Key did not keep hampering Chris with the issue, but Pastor Kee always suspected that his son may have stolen from him and his other son may be keeping quiet about it. In the video he does not talk about how Chris denied the allegations but I'm sure there is lingering disappointment and apprehension from either side. It is common for people to steal from others when it seems like they have an abundance and the materials taken are easily replaceable. However, it is not uncommon when a family with an expected moral standard accuses a child of deceit or thievery. Fast forward to 2017, Pastor Kee was preparing for another tour and gathering equipment at the studio. As he directed his younger son to pack the empty keyboard cases for the tour, he was surprised to find the actual keyboards in the case shells that he assumed had been empty and collecting dust in the studio. Pastor Kee discovered 10 Keyboards and four or so drum machines of different brands. The surprise feeling of finding these keyboards suddenly shifted to relief, then shame, finally landing on remorse. Pastor Kee realized he had made a mistake and went to YouTube to reconcile the error.

I am normally not a fan of people publicly posting personal business in the media unless there is something positive to be gained from the information shared. But in this circumstance, I was more impressed and proud to have encountered John P. Kee after seeing his apology than I was when he wrote me a three-thousand-dollar check. Pastor Kee apologized in three distinct ways that were poignant for me. First, he apologized to his son Chris for being wrong in his accusation and asked for his forgiveness. Second, he apologized for thinking that his son would steal from him. I'm sure it was difficult for Chris to experience the negative portrayal of him in his dad's mind. Lastly, Pastor Kee repented to God for making this false accusation. As a result of being a Pastor and God-fearing man, he had the conviction to make it right with his son, the public, and his father in heaven, holding his actions to a higher standard. Even if you are a non-believer, it's not difficult to admire Pastor Kee's efforts and the magnitude of his remorse. As fathers and parents, we can mend many relationships by admitting our mistakes and going back to reconcile a troubling issue that is dormant but not dead to the person who has trespassed against us. Pastor Kee provided an example that all leaders and parents can duplicate to improve relationships and self-integrity.

Chapter 5

FATHER TO FATHER CONNECTION

Let's talk about the beauty of children connecting with their father and grandfather. It is amazing when a child can garner wisdom from two tiers of experience and guidance. Wisdom is wealth that can be shared with the younger generation and sometimes we do not understand the value of it until we witness someone who is living life without this support of erudition. A family can be three generations of doctors, educators, engineers, military members, or entertainers. No matter the label, we should always take pride in our family carrying a label that is positive and productive, as there are family's that are known for crooked business dealings and deceit. When assessing a person, it is rarely on their individual merit. When I underwent a background investigation for my federal job, I was asked a lot of questions that had to do with my family and their social and career standing. When a person is getting married, most people want to know about the family they are marrying into and their history. Bad behaviors can filter down from generation to generation like a flow of water running down a quiet stream.

In his collection, *The Mishomis Book*, Edward Benton-Banai documents traditional teachings and principles that are beneficial in our modern-day societies. Specifically, Benton-Banai talks about Seven teachings that should be passed along from father to father, or to the leader of the household. These teachings are derived from the Anishinaabe people who are a native community in Canada and northern regions of North America. Many Anishinaabe societies still hold the Grandfather or eldest male family member in highest regard. Several believe that philosophical insights and life direction should come from the male head of the tribe. It is the duty of the highest-ranking member of the family to provide the following seven teachings to the upcoming generation. Number one is wisdom, through experiences, knowledge, and displaying good judgment. Wisdom must be shared and preached from the grandparents to the grandkids. Everyone is encouraged to have their own experiences, of course, but the grandparents are expected to convey advice that will help the grandkids avoid a pitfall. Most bad things that happen to a person are avoidable.

Grandparents possess an arsenal of knowledge that can help to reduce negative outcomes for their grandkids.

I have witnessed my own mother give advice to my nephew, Christopher, whilst spelling out the options and possible results. She says things like, "Christopher, when your mother was your age, she decided to do this, and this is what happened. I advise you to do something different because I have seen this story before." The grandparents get to use their life experiences—instilled by their parents and grandparents— as well as their kid's life experience to benefit their own grandchildren.

The second teaching is love. This can be hard to detect at times among the baby boomer generation regarding how they raised generation X and Y. Referring to my earlier chapter, "Loving with your Hands," there is a high percentage of grandparents who did not actively practice this with their sons because they were focused on "toughening them up" and neglected physical bonding. However, it is healthy for grandparents to be affectionate with their grandchildren. As a loose example, the ultimate goal is for a consistent chain of love to have begun with the 70-year-old granddad by expressing that toward his 45-year-old son who then passes that love and affection on to his 20-year-old son without a break in the love link.

The third teaching highlighted among the Anishinaabe people is respect. There is a common saying, "Respect is not given it is earned," but that is a false statement. Respect should initially be extended to elders in the family and people who hold a title of authority or position. However, respect can disappear from a relationship when mistrust or harm of any kind manifests. Respect is a concept that needs to be taught to our kids, especially in this current social climate that readily challenges authority and traditional views. Another aspect of respect is self-respect. Behaving with dignity and self-worth is the responsibility of the elders to teach the youth. Establishing the foundation for what the family stands for and what behaviors are acceptable or not should be ingrained with the family values. Respecting diversity and acknowledging positive changes in world views, like increasing equality and the valuing of women and other civil rights. Respect is a gift that should be extended to everyone who has proven themselves worthy, contingent upon the possibility of it being revoked when the person proves themselves unworthy. Sons lose respect for their father, and daughters for their mother when the parent is hypocritical, selfish, manipulative, unstable, and non-protective. Respect is not something that can automatically sustain a two-way relationship without consistent work and maintenance from the elder member of the relationship.

The fourth lesson is bravery. Bravery is sometimes overused and misplaced when describing a person or situation. There are brave professions such as military service members, firefighters, police officers, and even coal miners. It is brave to stand up to someone who is attacking a helpless person. Rescuing someone from the hand of danger is brave. Parents are often brave when it comes to protecting their kids like a mama bear to her cubs. Nevertheless, my favorite display of bravery is standing up for the right cause even when it is unpopular or against the majority. Everyone is not brave even in the face of danger. There has to be some selflessness when performing a courageous act. Simple things as teaching our kids how, when, and why to speak up when they are presented with wrong information or witness harm being done to others.

There is a show called "What Would You Do?" on the ABC network that gives people a chance to be brave and show integrity during a staged scenario, though participants are unaware they're being filmed at the time. Bravery does not have any association with age, race, gender, or size. I recall when I was 11-years-old standing in front of a taco shop with my dad and siblings, and a woman fell to the ground while having a seizure. I did not know what was going on at the time; I thought this lady was transforming into something like in a scary movie, or just simply choking. My dad quickly cradled the woman in his arms and tried to stop her from biting or swallowing her tongue. He then yelled for someone to call the paramedics. I thought that was brave for my dad to jump right in and try to help or possibly save a stranger's life. There was no hesitation or second-guessing for him concerning what he felt was the right thing to do in that moment. The risk for my dad was minimal, but I do not think he would have shunned away either way. The lesson I learned later, and during the experience, was that it is impossible to swallow your own tongue, but it does hurt trying, and I also learned to care for others in need.

The fifth lesson is honesty. Honesty is difficult when it is not favorable for oneself. As parents, we are firm about our kids telling us the truth at all cost because it is challenging to help them if we do not have the complete picture. There are times when you need to be brave and honest. Some people live a life of dishonesty, in their relationships, or even by making a dishonest living. For example, there are a large number of individuals scamming honest people out of security deposits for homes and apartments by requesting they send funds online through untraceable sources such as MoneyGram; all the while, the person receiving the money has no legal right to rent or sell the property and has no intent on delivering anything whatsoever to the unsuspecting consumer. It's all an internet hoax with false claims. And if any of those scammers have children, I honestly don't know how they look them in the eye. You cannot be an indecent person and a decent leader of a home. All parents' should have a legacy that includes honesty in their children's eyes, even if it is uncomfortable or not glamourous. However, everything does not need to be disclosed to the child if it is not beneficial to the child's path. I respect the man who is responsible for cleaning office building bathrooms more than the man who wears a suit and tie but scams people out of their money.

Humility is lesson number six, and that requires practice via teaching by example. To instill humility in our children, we need to give thanks for the little things, and show appreciation for our abundance. Our titles and status are not always important and should not be the focal point of what defines a person. There are times to lead, and times to be lead. But when you are the lead, do not forget how you felt and acted when you were learning in the background. Humbleness and hunger are two great traits any humble person can possess. I observed early that a good shepherd smells like sheep because he has not distanced himself too far from the flock nor set himself above the pack. My mother is very accomplished but her ego is in check, per se. She remains approachable and grateful for every promotion or recognition. Our kids must know that grace comes to those who are humble.

Finally, truth. Operating in a truthful manner that you can live with should be important to all who care about integrity. It sounds simple, but many people have issues with not being true to their character or beliefs. It is good to teach our kids to be passionate about the things that are important to them and be steadfast with that decision. Peer pressure is a device that is used to bend our trueness to self. It is okay to be the outlier or outcast if you are sticking to self-principles. People who protest are individuals who are staying true to their cause or belief. When our kids are entering into the adolescent stage they are still searching for their identity and most times need help in what defines them as young people and how they can stick to who they are at that moment. As parents, we must recognize in our kids that everyone is not called to do the same thing because we all have different talents and various measures of those talents. However, the structure of who we are must correlate with those talents. All of these principles should be filtered down from grandfather to grandchildren.

It is interesting sometimes when a family gets together, and the different generations are interacting. At times, the grandparent is observing how their grandkids are developing. When a grandparent sees an action or trait in a grandchild that they disapprove of they are often quick to say, "I don't know where you learned that from," or "We need to talk to your parents about that behavior." There are two ways to dissect this thought. First, grandparents are supposed to check the work of the parents and hold them accountable to the family principles if those things have proven to benefit the child's interest. Yes, times have changed, and our society has relaxed the acceptable standard of many things, but family principles cannot yield to the external environment. Whatever systems were laid out for the family, are still for the family. The seven teachings previously mentioned cannot waiver with generations. Parents need accountability, even with their kids, and it is unfortunate if the grandparents do not qualify to provide that assistance.

Grandfathers were designed to be the patriarch—the person who is the great counselor possessing traditional wisdom and spiritual guidance. Wisdom has to be passed down; it is not a gift that is given to everyone once they reach age 60. There are still some unadvised and immature seniors.

It is unfortunate when a grandparent disqualifies themselves as being a positive influence in their grandkid's life because they cannot mend relationships with the grandchild's parent or shake their own poor behavior. Father to father connection is about linking right behaviors or responses and disconnecting the bad habits. Perfecting a new path is like bypass heart surgery, particularly avoiding blockage and bad history digested over the years. After years of poor communication and dishonesty from a parent, those elements build up and disrupt the flow of a family. Many families are uncomfortable talking about tragedies or faults of the past and present. In families, you can find tragedies of domestic molestation, abuse, neglect, and mistreatment. These things shape our kid's path and perspective, sometimes permanently. Failure to address family transgressions such as these create more blockage. The cardiologist has to first examine and detect where the plaque is building up in the artery. Plaque disrupts blood flow to the heart and increases the chance of a heart attack. Turmoil in a family cannot stay hidden forever before it disrupts the family's cohesiveness.

The process of bypassing family blockage takes

communication and all necessary parties to admit their mistakes without justification. After a major procedure like bypass surgery, the recovery time is 12 weeks, and it is a significantly higher risk when the procedure is in an emergency case, or when the patient has other illnesses. After repairing a family issue, give it time for things to get back to normal and begin again with healthy habits. Do not wait for an emergency to happen to address an existing issue; it will increase the chances of an adverse outcome. Most significantly it is the charge of the Patriarch or Matriarch to be the mender of broken relationships for it is their responsibility to leave the family in a better condition for when they pass on. Grandparents and great-relatives help create new paths back to the center of health and positive movement.

Chapter 6

BLOOD IS THICKER THAN WATER BUT NOT THICKER THAN LOVE

"Love recognizes no barriers. It jumps hurdles, leaps fences, and penetrates walls to arrive at its destination full of hope."
– Maya Angelou

I dedicate this Chapter to the men and women who raise kids that are not biologically related or may not share the last name of the child they are raising. I am a fan of foster parents, step parents or anyone who made a choice to love and protect our little ones. Kids need attention, guidance, protection, love; but they do not need to share the same bloodline as the one who is committed to fulfilling a promise of parenthood. Love is a powerful word that requires manifestation through action and commitment. I fell in love with a two-year-old girl named Dylan over 12 years ago. I met Dylan when she was nine months old, but married her mom when Dylan was two. Dylan did not have my eyes, lips, or personality. Dylan did not possess any feature to trace her back to me but what we had was an opportunity to create and nurture a new relationship. I became a step-parent, and it was not hard since Dylan's biological father was not present and skirting his responsibilities because he had moved on with another family at that time. In my experience, parenting is more difficult when there is a bridge of adoption or step-parenting to cross. The relationship between the new parent and child needs to form authentically. It would be wrong of me to marry Dylan's mother without accepting Dylan. However, the adjustment period was tough for all parties, including Dylan's mother, who struggled with different parenting styles and allowing for correction to come from a source other than herself.

Many step-parents have a difficult time establishing the right pace and method for making the blended family healthy and functional. I always say it starts with the adult because the adult should have the mental capacity for patience, care, understanding, and unity. I did make my mistakes with Dylan because she was three-years-old and used to having her mom's undivided attention and probably more relaxed house rules. I came into the picture thinking I was bringing more structure, but a three-year-old kid does not understand. The beauty in the forming of Dylan's and my relationships is that she started to pick up phrases that I said around the house and little acts that I thought were funny. We began to build our own rapport that did not have to include her mom. The cool thing about being a step-parent is when the kid does something moronic, we blame the behavior on the absent parent. When Dylan began to jump on my lap because she wanted my attention, I knew I was doing something right. When Dylan became an older sister to her brother David Jon, I consciously kept making an effort with Dylan so that she did not ever feel that she was second best. Even though my relationship with Dylan and David Jon's mother did not last, our love for each other has remained steadfast. I'm in love with my kids. My sacrifice and commitment are not based on credit or validation from outsiders. I parent because kids make me complete. Teaching, mentorship, mutual love, and reproduction of the family are what make life great over the course of its evolution. Many parents do not use terms such as step-dad or even mother-in-law. Removing the "step" out of stepdad is similar to shifting from father to daddy. When it comes to parenting, I want parents to try to eliminate any barriers between the child and the parent so love can reside.

The most amazing people to walk the earth are couples who decide to adopt a child. Yes, adoption is a selfless act, but the hurdles to conquer in the adoption process demonstrate the devotion to love an innocent child who experienced rejection or was unable to be cared for by their biological family. During the adoption process, there is a home study fee established by state social workers, including their attorney fees, which are all part of the cost to take on the responsibility of becoming a parent. Parents who adopt are paying to become a parent, which will cost them even more time and money. Several adults choose not to have kids or avoid the responsibility of giving time, money, and attention to the child they created. Everyone knows that children cost money, but couples seeking adoption are willing to pay large sums to ensure that the child gets a loving home and the healthy life experiences that they deserve. There are kids in the system who were not neglected by their parents; instead, due to death, or other misfortunes, those children are disconnected from their natural family. Adoption processes vary based on whether the parents are adopting internationally, domestically, and then through a private adoption agency or the state, all the while adhering to state policies. Many successful people have excelled in life with adopted parents. Two former United States Presidents and two former United States First Ladies were adopted by family members or strangers. Steve Jobs, co-founder of Apple Inc., singers Faith Hill and Sarah McLachlan, and legendary baseball player Babe Ruth became successful out of an adopted family environment. Love can propel a child to heights that are unimaginable. The job of an adopted parent is to love the child through their differences and conquer the insecurities the child may experience through love. Lack of trust causes hindrance in a relationship, and ensuring a child whole-heartedly feels like they will not continue to experience abandonment is hard for an adopted parent. Yes, there are many scenarios for adoptive families and how they came together. However, it is the same principle across the board, love the children and be honest and forthcoming on both sides. The adult has to be willing to go one step beyond to get the most out of the child.

Can you love the kid who does not look like you?
Can you love the child through nightmares, even when they seem to have a problem with you?
The child who does not share any interest of yours
The kid who wears a frown when you attempt to pull out more
Your friends who doubted the choice to take this journey on
Can you push through adversity for the child to feel they belong?
The thoughts and fear to fail or not feel accepted
Both sides of the coin do not want to be rejected
Or neglected by the one who chose them out of the group
Selecting someone who does not resemble any of your fruit?
Your heart must be big and in the right place
Willing to exhaust your resources and energy for smile on the face
Not taking offense when the child grows up to seek its originator

FROM FATHER TO DADDY

For the void is theirs to fill like an empty refrigerator
Knowing that your job was to give the child a chance
And to give the gift of love every day in abundance
For your heart and deed, you are now blessed
To experience the love that is greater than the rest
It does feel good knowing you raised a stud
But I bet it feels better learning love is thicker than blood
By David A. White

Giving a child up for adoption does not mean the mother gave up on the child. Everyone's story is unique and should be considered on a case-by-case basis. The bond between a mother and baby is almost unbreakable. I have been fortunate enough to be in the delivery room for both of my sons' birth. It would be close to impossible to carry a human in my belly for almost ten months, transforming my body and diet to say goodbye for good on the day I deliver. At the same time, it can be viewed as selfless when a mother makes that heart-breaking decision to give the child up because they feel they cannot support the child's needs and give the child the best chance at life. Some would say all the kid needs is love, but love sometimes is tangible and manifests into time, money, and attention. If a mother is overwhelmed, how can she demonstrate her love other than words? My wife can tell me she loves me every day, but some actions must happen for me to feel that she does love me. There is a certain level of attention and sacrifice I want to see to prove that love. Love for a child has to be accompanied by action not just words. Kids will be left wondering if their parents love them if the parent never comes to any performance or never instigates one-on-one activities with them. Also, taking mental and emotional health into consideration, kids need a mother who is mentally stable, and has a support group or mechanism that does not negatively impact the child. Adoption has saved millions of lives, and the mother who had the sense to relinquish their precious responsibility can be called rational. However, it can be complicated to see any winners in an adoption scenario until the child reaches full adult status with the correct and healthy understanding of why they were put up for adoption, and how they benefited in the end.

Although children are looking for parental warmth, love can come from many directions. When there is a child who lacks love and attention, adults playing various roles in the child's life can step up to the plate. Attention goes a long way. Children are referred to as little people because they need the same things that grown/big people need. Kids who lack love and attention do have a different physiological reaction than those who are given time and attention by a loving caregiver. Why would a kid have the desire to do "right" if no one cares whether they do or not or how they turn out? The role of a school teacher, coach, community director, and school counselor is critical in identifying the warning signs from kids who do negative things for attention. Everyone needs somebody in their corner to help them stay on the path of success. There are many stories of coaches taking kids into their home and overseeing the child's athletic pursuits through high school or college. The coach not only saw the athletic potential in the child but recognized the child's need for a caring leader to help in ensuring the child reached their highest potential. Jason Crutchfield was Claressa Shields (the 2012 and 2014 American Female Olympian Boxing Champion) coach, and he helped her get to the professional competition level. Jason stepped up when Claressa's parents were unable to support her, and Claressa ended up staying with Crutchfield and his wife. Jason obviously went beyond the duty of a coach, but he knew what Claressa needed, and Claressa responded positively with great success. Investing confidence, hope, love, and discipline in a child will always earn a positive return. Coaches like Jason are not there to take the place of the parents but sometimes bridge the gap until the parent can step back into their rightful place, or until the child can support themselves without being dependent on their parents. Everyone is built differently, but, after a long period of neglect, most people can become self-sufficient and function at a fairly high level without parental backup; however, this is not optimal. A coach or teacher cannot replace a parent, but the attention and love from them can catapult a child to their destiny of success.

Coaching do not have to be limited to competitive coaching either. As adults, there are kids young and old who can use a life coach or at least some attention and confidence boosters from time to time.

I recently had a friend named Jock who had fallen upon hard times. By age 32, both of his parents and grandparents were deceased. Jock's relationship with his parents was incomplete—not just because some life success principles were missing, but time had run out before he could figure out his adult path. As a friend, and parent who is well-aware of the type of support and encouragement people need to succeed, I stepped in and provided that attention and hope for Jock. Jock did not have a healthy relationship with any other family members and had become homeless and out of a job. I could sense suicide on Jock's mind. It is crushing to a person's self-esteem and value when their world flips upside down and all of a sudden it appears that no one cares about their existence. I put Jock up in a motel a few times, but most importantly I provided encouraging words and a plan for him to use his talents to dig himself out of this ditch.

Sometimes a person's own flesh and blood will not support them, instead neglecting them in a time of need. However, I have a love for humanity in general, and like my father before me I want to convey that to my children as well through action. Most people in distress need a person with the mental fortitude to redirect them, instill confidence, principles, and a way forward. People that are enduring hardship do not always need financial relief: they often require more education and training. People tend to avoid individuals dealing with hardship because they often think the situation is going to require a financial burden to rectify, but the best gift is always knowledge. My parents taught me to love family and also love people. Everyone is not fortunate to have basic needs met like safety, love, and parental guidance. Love can penetrate some of the most tragic and disarray circumstances. Whether a stepparent, adoptive parent, or coach, we can deliver a healthy form of love to the developing minds in our care, with the intent to make our world a better place, and with the hope that the individuals we convey that love to will pay it forward as well.

Chapter 7

A Father's Sacrifice

When most people think about the life of a parent the word sacrifice is at the top of the list. We understand how much the mother sacrifices when it comes to changing the diet, body shape, and putting career or schooling on hold for extended periods of time for the sake of the child and family. But what about the father's sacrifice? Yes, dad may have to request more hours at the job or seek a higher paying job. Sacrificing is not always attached to financial means or use of time, though. Sometimes as fathers we have to sacrifice our pride, ego, and will for our child. For a dad, surrendering ego can be more complicated than money. It was not until I understood this type of sacrifice that I was able to have the optimal relationship between myself and my son's mother. My eldest sons' mom and I separated and divorced when he was only three-years-old. His mother and I were committed to exchanging him on the weekends, sometimes for weeks at a time when he was not yet school age. We had a mutually agreed upon system in place to make the best of our circumstances.

For the last eight years, we have met at the halfway point between San Diego (where I live) and Los Angeles (where she resides). The halfway point is Mission Viejo, Orange County, California which is 60 miles one way. For the majority of the eight years, we would meet Friday night and exchange again Sunday Afternoon every other weekend. One weekend would cost me 240 miles of wear and tear and a full tank of gas. A whole year cost me 6,240 miles of wear and tear, 26 full tanks of gas, and an oil change. The last eight years have cost 49,920 miles, more than several tanks of gas, oil changes, and countless hours of sitting in traffic on the Interstate 5 Highway. For my son's mother and I, it is equal sacrifice and commitment to making sure our son gets time with both parents. Yes, there were some Friday night events I could not attend because it was my weekend, and I missed countless Sunday afternoon professional football games because we were doing an exchange in Orange County.

The consequence that I did not foresee was a blend of sacrifice and loss that comes with not raising my child in the same household as his mother. My lack of in-person interaction with my son Monday-Thursday made my influence on him less than what I anticipated or desired. By the time my son was seven-years-old, he also had many of his mother's characteristics. It makes sense that my son would pattern some of his ways after his mom because he's spending the majority of his time with her. But at that time, I would get upset with my son's mom about what she was allowing him to do. However, when I think back on it, her ways were not that harmful. Like most fathers, I would ask my son how was school going? Does anyone pick on you? If someone ever does, make sure you stand up for yourself. My son's mother's message would be different, instructing him to tell the teacher or an adult if someone was picking on him. There are some social consequences that happens when parents are raising the same child out of two different houses with two separate sets of rules. It is not fair to get upset with the child who is doing what is allowed in the other household, nor is it fair to get upset with the other parent who has their own philosophies and isn't necessarily upholding yours. It is fair to understand the situation for what it truly is and know that as the part-time or half-time parent your imprint on the child will be sacrificed. As a dad who has shared custody I had to swallow my pride and communicate more behind the scenes with my son's mother on how we can be—if not on the same page, at least in the same chapter. The sooner I accepted there would be a slight difference from what I intended for my son, the less stressful our job as co-parents became.

As co-parents, the time with your children should not include trying to erase what the other parent is teaching, allowing, or introducing to your child. All of the work such as planning and communicating must happen on the front end between the parents and often. Co-parents must make time for each other to discuss the progress of the child and what they both want for the child. The difficulty is in the methods that the parents want to use. As a co-parent, we should discover each other's strengths and embrace those powers for the parent to have a successful role in the child's life. I did not like it all the time when my son would stay the weekend, and he had two hours' worth of homework or Kumon math problems. My son's mother would get upset with me if the work was not at least 80 percent finished. Yes, the homework cut into son and father time, but this was important to his mother and beneficial to my son's education down the road.

When David Jon reached 10-years-old, I wanted him to play youth sports to help him develop a competitive spirit and social bond with kids his age. David Jon's mother was not interested in making that time commitment and required me to be at every other game which was 130 miles away from me one way. Once again, my son's mother recognized how important it was to me for David Jon to participate in youth sports at that time in his life for there are benefits and life lessons that are derived from team sports. Co-parents have to honor each other's desires and input for the child they share. No parent has all the ingredients to shape a perfect child, but I do know that four hands are better than two, and what has worked for me is embracing each other's ideas as co-parents. It is a sacrifice because all ideas may not approve. Relinquishing some decision-making, possibly to the stepparent, is hard to do, but the concern should always be what's best for the child, not whose idea it was.

There is a stigma that male parents are apprehensive about displaying love via emotion and affection in the presence of their kids. I know dads who show how passionate they are about their children through dominant personality traits. There may be a parent who shows their passion through physical touch or the angry father who tells everyone, "Don't mess with my kid or I'll mess you up!" I have observed many fathers yelling at their kid's coach or even threatening the child's mother in the name of "love" for their son. The child that witnesses this behavior from their dad is not saying to themselves, "Oh, see how much my dad loves me." The child thinks, "My old man is a nut." Let's not be the father whose love is compounded with fear and anger. Males parents, who are dominant creatures by nature, need to start digging deeper into our tool belt to get things resolved, peacefully inching closer to the result we desire. In the great Denzel Washington movie *John Q*, Denzel's character is a passionate father who held the hospital hostage until they placed his son on the priority list for heart donors.

The father in this movie had also sold most of his possessions to try to raise money for the heart procedure for his son. Most Dads think they have the same passion as John Q and many of us do. We work jobs that we do not like or receive adequate appreciation for because of the love and sacrifice for our family.

As fathers, there are times our value is the sacrifice in our home. It seems like fathers are always second to know, and last to receive credit. I am not always able to make the school programs or awards, but I still want to know what is going on with my children. My work schedule and other financial ventures have put me in a position to make sure that the cash flow is sufficient for us all to live a particular lifestyle. It hurts me as a dad not to receive the invite to my kid's award ceremony because my son's mother assumes I cannot make the event. As parents, sometimes the sacrifice is having to disappoint your kids because they do not understand that if you do not meet this work deadline or work shift, we are all moving in with grandma. Even in a co-parenting situation, there has to be some grace, mercy, and understanding for when the other parent does not come through. Sacrifice comes from many directions, but sometimes communication with the child is appropriate, so everyone is on the same page. Sacrifice is sometimes being there, and sometimes not being there and looking like the dad that is too busy. There has to be understanding; furthermore, a balance. Payday cannot always supersede playdates.

As young fathers, finding balance always seems to be a struggle. On the day I turned 30 years old, I had plans to go out with a special girl I was interested in dating. I had a nice budget for the date, and a babysitter lined up for my youngest son, Isaiah. Isaiah's mom and I were no longer a couple, and she was active-duty military deployed. The birthday plan was to pick up my toddler son Isaiah from daycare, go home, change, and drop Isaiah off with the babysitter while daddy goes out for a night of fun. When I arrived at the daycare, they told me Isaiah had seemed "out of it" since lunch, and he might be coming down with an illness. I took Isaiah to the car, and as soon as I lifted him to place him in his car seat, he threw up all over my shirt. He looked lethargic and was apologetic. Right then my daddy instincts started kicking in, and I knew I could not take my son to a babysitter in this condition. Turning 30-years-old should be celebrated, and I was excited to go out with this girl who was always making and breaking plans with me. I sent her a text and let her know that I was unavailable for my birthday date because my child was ill. I never did get a make-up date with her, but that is part of the sacrifice that parents make. Fathers make the same sacrifices as mothers when it comes to our children. Freedom is surrendered when you become a parent. There are many stories of parents charged with child endangerment because they left the kids at home while they went somewhere to party. I have also heard extreme cases of both parents agreeing to let a 12-year-old and six years old care for themselves while the parents make a two-day trip to Las Vegas. When you have kids early, sometimes you have to forfeit the opportunities to party, which is part of the parental sacrifice. Child endangerment, selfishness, and poor judgment cannot be justified or excused when a child's safety is at risk.

If fathers would sacrifice more, what would things look like for the family? I want to avoid the standard American way. Work a job for 30 to 40 years then retire after giving 33 percent of that time to my career and probably 15 percent of my time to family. I am on the grind to break the usual way. I am going to knock down every promotion door, get certifications, degrees, and not be complacent or satisfied with retiring with 80 percent of my salary at age 64. The thing about sacrifice is projecting how each particular sacrifice is going to gain equity or have a purpose as a positive result. As parents, our sacrifices have to be meaningful and strategic. I do not want to put my relationship with the family in danger, but I also do not want to jeopardize my career or other lucrative opportunities. Some things will have the short-term payoff and others long-term. Routine tasks can be disrupted for family always! Fathers would look like the hero with their family if they knew that you choose them as the priority. Fathers, we have to donate time, money, attention, advice, leadership and strength to our families. If someone has to die in the family from sleep deprivation or exhaustion, let be me, I'm the daddy. Sacrifice is in our job description as dads; I recall a time when

I was scheduled to meet my son's mother to exchange him for the weekend. I was stressed because my finances were low during this period. I did not have enough money for gas, or entertainment and food. I even thought about writing a bad check to cover some expenses. Things did not resort to any bad behavior, but I took a chance and met for the exchange anyhow. David Jon's mom could tell that my countenance was down. She asked me what was wrong, and I burst into tears of shame. I said I was resistant to doing the exchange that weekend because I did not have enough money to even buy our son a meal. She immediately became hushed but firm and asked me to follow her to the gas station. She filled up my gas tank and gave me forty dollars. I had sacrificed my pride and exposed myself to the women who I was supposed to show that I was doing better without her. I learned two valuable lessons right then. First, I cannot let my pride interrupt the flow of my relationships that benefit my children. Second, co-parenting, even with an ex-wife or girlfriend, should always operate in a civil manner for the interest of the child or children.

In most cases, people want to project discord toward an ended relationship, but I know it is best to always care for each other when there is childcare involved. When Isaiah's mom left the military after serving 15 years, there was an adjustment period when her mind and emotions were fragile. I had to show empathy toward her concerning that even though she was not my woman and I belonged to someone else because if she was not okay then Isaiah was not okay. Mental health is a significant concern for all, and as a non-clinician, I do not know who is struggling with what issues. I do know that I can do my part in being concerned for the well-being of people who interact with and can impact my child. If I am feeling emotionally fragile, I need to speak up and say I need a break from my son to work on me. Support systems are necessary to depend on; everyone needs assistance at some point. With my son's mother, peace had to be the forefront of our relationship, and this comes through sacrificing of ego, control, and willingness to be wrong and own it. Why are so many levels of sacrifice required? It all has to do with the love we have for our kids and the choice to making their world better. We must show our children that one of the primary ways to show love is to sacrifice.

Chapter 8

FATHERHOOD IMPACTS EVERYTHING

Does fatherhood impact criminal behavior? Yes, directly and indirectly. Juvenile offenders live by ruthless and reckless rules, and in most cases the father's presence and guidance were absent. Teenagers act out in disturbing ways when upset with a parent, especially when dealing with rejection from a parent, or cannot be managed by a parent. Does fatherhood impact a son or daughter's self-esteem? Damn right! Yes, it is natural for all girls to want to be their father's princess or baby girl. When that feeling of being valued is missing, some girls turn into women looking for a man to make her their baby girl. A boy desires to make his dad proud and show off his growing strength and development. It's hard for any child not to hear you've done me proud but males can be prideful creatures and sometimes we are the last ones to know that what we missed from our father has impacted our self-esteem. Does fatherhood affect how a person shows or receives love? Yes, people have to be taught how to love, especially if it is something unfamiliar. I remember when Dylan was three-years-old and she met her infant brother David Jon, we had to tell her how to touch him: "Please, Dylan, do not be rough and only touch and kiss him." Some women do not know how a man should treat them because they did not receive a healthy example of respect from their father. Other women may have witnessed their father cheat, lie, neglect, or abuse their mother, causing a flawed perspective on male and female interaction. Some kids grow to be adults who are not comfortable in a relationship that has constant physical touch because they are not accustomed to loving with your hands or perhaps have experienced unwelcome contact.

Father's help their children find their voice and purpose. My dad taught me to work hard and be a reliable worker. My father did not call in sick because he wanted to stay out with his friends longer. I saw my dad and uncles go to work with sleep in their eyes numerous times. Kids do benefit from watching their parents work an honest hard career. Kids have a gift to detect instability at an early age. Children can tell if their parent or parents are not stable. A guardian that is always moving homes, careers, or relationships, inserts imbalance in a child's mind. There are too many adults with lazy work ethics, choosing to golf, play video games, or enjoy tea time with girls instead of busting their butt in school or a career. Each generation is supposed to raise the bar, particular within the family. Fathers influence their kids on how to pursue happiness for themselves and loved ones.

The impact fathers have on the child's psychological well-being, and social behavior has been evident for many years and is widely statistically documented. In this book, the reoccurring theme is investing in your kids socially and doing everything possible to avoid known or unknown maltreatment. When a loving father is not in the home, the children are susceptible to abuse of some form or another. The child loses the natural protector from child predators. The presence of a father provides a sense of protection and safety. Currently, the single mother statistic is extremely high. Some data says around 40% of homes are without a father. However, there are many reasons for this staggering number. Mothers are living with their boyfriend unmarried, and that contributes to the data. Many ex-wives petition for primary or full physical custody, and the family court systems are designed to award child rights to women. Many times, fathers are not afforded the right even to be a presence for their kids. Even though a household with a father is less likely to live in poverty or abuse drugs, women opt to run the home without our assistance. Becoming a single mother can be by choice in some cases. More women entertain the idea of raising kids without a partner or man because they do not have time to endure another failed relationship. A person has the right to raise a child as the sole guardian. Some women discover that they are ready to be a parent before being a wife. Or a successful woman may reach the end of her reproductive years, and the maternal clock is ticking, but she has no desire to make a relationship commitment with an adult life-partner.

Sperm donors have been around for years but what is the aftermath? There are many causes for a family or women to use a fertility clinic for impregnation. The donors typically are screened for STDs, genetic diseases, and undergo comprehensive testing. Unfortunately, there have been horror stories involving the fertility doctors implanting their semen in women. Also, there was a story about a mentally-disturbed man lying on his application, and his sperm was used to impregnate over 35 women successfully. Those kids now have a higher risk of developing a mental illness as they mature. Even a seemingly clear path to conception can come with its own obstacles. Whichever path a person chooses, having a kid is the most precious responsibility that requires a significant amount of thought. Deciding who will share the biological and psychological demands of parenting requires careful consideration. Not only do genetic issues carry over but mental challenges will surface at some point. Sperm donors do come with some ethical issues as well because, at some point, the parent risks the child possibly feeling incomplete because of never knowing one of their biological parent's. We live in a society now where life can be created through medical intervention rather than natural methods. Yes, as a society, we have been able to circumvent the system of "Mother Nature," but is there collateral damage happening as a result? On the one hand, we should be thankful for the advancements in medicine that help preserve and repair life, and even help to create it, bringing fulfillment and joy to a family.

Life is not fair when a family who is prepared in every imaginable way to welcome a child into this world, biologically cannot; yet the couple who was not trying, and is unappreciative of the gift, easily conceives. A single mother who chooses to go the route of fertile implantation such as via a sperm bank must be aware of the aftermath. There is a disadvantage as a single parent compounded with the child not knowing their full identity and wanting answers at some point. The truth is everyone does not deserve to bear fruit, but everyone deserves to give love and be loved. Bless the single parent who chooses to go against the odds and welcome the trials of creating life and loving the creation in spite of it being a purposeful solo mission. There is no need to hide the truth from the kid, and especially not for medical reasons, but mostly because the truth does set a person free. Identity is an issue for everyone at some point in their life.

Fathers in the home are supposed to serve as a guide

to the outside world. A lot of people are or feel misguided because daddy was not there. Daddy issues apply to men just as they do to women. Women often get accused of making poor choices because they have "daddy issues." Unfortunately, there is some validity to the narrative. As I mentioned earlier in the chapter, every woman has an inner princess in them who wants to be recognized by their father. There are consequences when not meeting primary needs; even if they are social blended with emotional, we as people then look for counterfeits or other alternatives to satisfy the need. With men, resentment and displaced anger can negatively impact the development of boys becoming men.

Fortunately, we live in a society where we are free to choose who we love...for the most part. I look forward to total freedom around the world for people to love who they choose without torment, ridicule or loss of family and friend support structures, which also contribute to creating healthier living environments for children. I am still personally a fan of a "traditional" family structure. However, protecting and providing for a child can be achieved by one or two adults of the same sex. Same-sex parents seem to have high success rates in positive child-rearing lately because they planned for the child, and the heterosexual couple may have stumbled upon parenting by accident.

That said, there are a considerable number of heterosexual women choosing to raise children alone. Setting same-sex family units aside, I present the question: Have fathers failed so much in the last 50 years that society has decided our role or place is not that unique? There are still many fathers who are trying to hit the ball out of the park. My intention is to rejuvenate, remind, repurpose, or reintroduce fathers and parents to planning out the best path for our little ones. Yes, some of the best families are not even blood-related or have a male presence in them, but that does not negate the impact fathers have on the family. A lot of dismantling of families is because daddy could not get his priorities, addictions, or lifestyle together. Fathers have screwed up for generations, operating with outdated methods, not anticipating their own impact on the household. The man was told to bring home the bacon while mama cooked it, but what about the shared attention to the kids? An amendment to the way we do business as the man of the household is in order. The forefathers founded our government, but after a while, revising and rewriting policies to fit the evolved standards and well-being of the commonwealth was inevitable for our evolution and progress. The same goes for fathers and their role in the home. My intent as a father and author is always to bring value and pride to the word "fatherhood," with the hope that even just one person can reconnect with their family while cutting down the weeds in their relationship and making room for new growth.

CONCLUSION

Reflecting on these principles has also prepared me to be more focused than ever before to lead with love. This single principle is the guiding force behind all others and is what all parents need to learn and practice. Preparation is the key to everything. When opportunity meets preparation, two crucial ingredients are in place for champions to emerge from both sides: the children and parents. Some people do not prepare for the big stage, the last two minutes of a competitive game, an impromptu speech or presentation to close a deal. When it comes to evolving into a great parent, we lead on the field and in the lesson room. Some team leaders are not vocal and just let their play and work ethics speak for themselves; unfortunately, that is not the best way to lead your kids. Children need to hear and experience the love us parents have for them. A child at eight-years-old is not going to understand that dad worked overtime this weekend so the family can have more of what they need to survive. Working extra hours is a testament to the father's love in a man's eyes. An eight-year-old or even 12-year-old is not always going to make the connection on why daddy works so many hours. The child just sees and understands that daddy is not there, and some kids resent their parent's job because they are competing for the time and attention of mom or dad. Every parent should take their child to work when appropriate so the child can preview an adult work environment. There are some things about the parental world that can be beneficial for sharing and this is one of them. I tell my kids I love them so much that I wake up at 5:30 a.m. to report to this building to perform these tasks until 4 p.m. Let our kids hear and see how our love plays a part in why we work so hard. Love connections are not just for adults; we have to make a connection with our children as well.

I do recognize that there is a significant amount of adult kids who are not connected or do not have the desired relationship with their parents. As we getter old, we start seeing our mother or father for who they are as a man or woman in the world. It is not illogical to find issues with who they are in their non-parental persona. There are things that we can discover in life about the person who cared for us that should not change our ideology of the quality of care we received. Some parents hide their smoking habits from their kids, and when the children find out they may be upset, but it does not expunge a job well done by the father. Sometimes we have to separate the actor from the character he or she plays. I'm not saying parenting is acting, but to a certain extent, it is. Adults have to act responsible, mature, caring, and patient in the presence of our kids and other children even though we are not always that way or do not feel like that all of the time. In corporate America, I put on a front for my coworkers in the sense of always being polite and patient. At home, I am not always courteous and patient. I use a vocabulary that is not appropriate for work. I can be assertive and aggressive in trying to develop solutions concerning things that impact my happiness. Could my coworkers handle every aspect of me? I think not. Shielding components of our personal lives are more common than not. There are some things about me that I want to keep private from the public and even my kids. Maintaining privacy is not for perverted or evil actions to go unknown. Privacy is important because people often cannot handle the full truth of who a person may be, especially because people have a hard time separating personal flaws from someone's professional accomplishments. Granted, there are times when the two cannot be separated because of the potential for harm being done to others, but that's not what I'm referring to in this context.

I recently encountered some imperfections and flaws in my father that may have been behind-the-scenes "pre-existing issues" for him. In my childhood days, my siblings and I did not detect a problem with my father that could have directly impacted us. Secrets can kill a family, especially if it involves bringing harm to others of any sort. Privacy does not mean secrecy and parents are people who deserve privacy from their kids. As an adult, presented with a struggle or concern that my father had years ago, and for me, it does not impact his good deeds as a father and should not. When a child reaches full maturity, they learn to have compassion for their parents' "blemishes." Love and compassion have to move in two directions at some point in the relationship between child and parent. It is possible, and sometimes necessary, to accept a father's work while condemning or rejecting their flaws and "demons" as a man. Many sports heroes do a hall-of -fame worthy job on the field but are revealed to be a wreck in their personal life. Some personal accomplishments and personal defects have no correlation in the matter. Lance Armstrong has done good and bad on the road and off. He did bring popularity to competitive cycling on a world Olympic stage, but he brought disgrace to that sport with allegations of doping which he admitted to later. In the midst of that development, Lance brought awareness to cancer prevention and raised millions of dollars for research. Lance has excelled as a philanthropist and an advocate for cancer-research foundations, which will be part of his legacy. As fans, we can choose what we want to remember and ignore concerning a person's positive and adverse behaviors. What Lance did in terms of the doping was done in secret with the intent to deceive for personal gain. Parents who withhold characteristic insecurities, or parts of themselves that could be interpreted in a less favorable light, are not causing harm. If something from a mother's past resurfaces, the ability to separate the two facets of the person is required. Capacity to separate the man and the father is also required. When a child becomes a parent, they should understand people can only do their best and sometimes their best lacks education and training.

I took my Son Isaiah to the barbershop at the tender age of three for the first time. I received many compliments on how well behaved he was sitting in the barber's chair. A barbershop is a unique place for me, and the African American culture. The barbershop is like a country club where you come to socialize, receive a service, and catch up with old friends and even colleagues. However, at a barbershop, people have more of a competitive spirit, defending their points on topics ranging from sports to laws. Similar to a country club, none of the customers want to be embarrassed by an action of their children. When the barber has a child in their chair that is misbehaving, moving or crying throughout the haircut process, it becomes incredibly frustrating for the barber. The barber is internally furious, and everyone in the shop talks about that kid and parent as soon as they leave. It is normal to expect a toddler to resist the barber because of a fear of being cut, controlled, and even the sound of the clippers in a young child's ear can be frightening. Before taking both of my kids to the barbershop, I prepared them. I first let them watch me get my haircut a number of times so they could see it's a simple, non-harmful process. Then I started off letting them hold the clippers when I shaved my hair at times at home. Once they became comfortable with that tool, they slowly let me trim their hair at home before handing them over to the professionals. By the time we went to the barbershop they were already comfortable, and well relaxed because the new challenge became not to fall asleep in the barber's chair. As parents, conquering fear is a huge element in success and paving a smooth path for the child.

My simple barbershop process can be broken down from different angles, but the key point, once again, is preparation. Constant education and training always lead to positive results. Teach and educate at the child's level. The way to demonstrate to a 13-year-old is vastly different than how to show a three-year-old. I like to adopt "The Titration to the effect" which is to adjust it until it works or keep inching towards the solution because the answer is unknown. When I enter the bath or shower, I change the valve temperature until I am comfortable with the level. Drastic turning and abruptness can shock the body and cause more harm than good. Some parent finds themselves losing their cool and comfortable pace when handling their child's issues. My father admitted a mistake between his handling of my old brother. When my dad found out my brother was experimenting with Marijuana, he panicked and possibly overreacted through punishment and aggressive arguing. In the popular TV show "The Simpsons," Homer is always strangling Bart every time he does something outrageous to upset Homer. Tweaking is part of parenting, and we make an adjustment to change behaviors of our children that are not going to benefit our plan for them but what is in the best interest of the child. "Titration to effect" has to be accompanied by love and discipline. Discipline is not always

Homer-and-Bart-Simpson-like encounters. The best solution sometimes involves patience and paying close attention to what the child needs. My son is not me, and his wants are not mine; I have to allow my son to be the best version of himself with a concentration on building to be better.

There are a few ugly truths about the relationship between parent and child. First, some do not know what's in the best interest of their child because they are having a difficult time understanding what the best interest is for themselves as an adult. I dive into this topic more in my book *Rushing to Fail*. In which, I discuss how some parents are not qualified to be their child's role model. Nevertheless, the second ugly truth is the mental health side of the equation, which can prevent parents from succeeding in childrearing beyond their control. For years, mothers and fathers with mental illness become undone and have a difficult time handling their issues and stress because they do not have the fortitude or understanding to incorporate a child into the equation with balance. Some parents are going so horrifically far they are killing their kids because they do not know how to love them through the varied stages of chemical imbalance and chronic depression. Depression is a mental illness that requires medical attention. The mind is delicate, and a parent who was alright on Friday can lose focus come Monday. As adults and protectors of all kids, we have to intervene and speak up for the child who feels neglected or abused, especially because some children who are abused see no way out but death to themselves or the abuser. As a father, I try to stay vigilant in this regard concerning all relationships I encounter between parents and children. But also, I want to continually learn how I can do better as a dad and share my knowledge with those who can use the help.

Men possess a distinctly unique mentality and ways for working through issues. It naturally takes two to make a child, with the intent for the child to take away qualities, characteristics, and traits from both creators. The non-nuclear family structure can still succeed, but the efforts of a positive and active father figure in the home make growth and goals easier to achieve.

The father represents the other half of questions, styles to love, support, and a person to reference for unique wisdom and insights on the world. Plenty of individuals make it to adulthood without ever meeting or seeing a picture of their father, and they seem complete, often saying they are satisfied with the way their life played out with those who chose to be a part of it. I have even heard the theory that if a child does not know what they are missing, they never had it to lose in the first place. I have also heard people say, "I was not aware that my family was poor growing up until I had to become an adult and provide for myself." Yes, a child is blind to things and can be content without something because they never had it to begin with, but there comes a time when that child because an adult and questions arise, and they have to start answering questions and filling in the blanks for themselves. Our self-esteem will be affected by the things we choose to fill in those blanks. Many roll with the cards they are dealt and adapt to change, but people also like to live in the "what if?" Society can never accurately replace fathers. For the man does represent strength, security, pride, and calmness in troubled waters. For the dads and moms who can do better and choose not, shame on them. If this book is used to repair a damaged relationship or diminish a mother's self-agenda so that their child can have a relationship with the father under healthy conditions, well-done, mother, you have advanced in your maturity. Guiding our kids with love, patience, and experience is the best investment we can make in their tomorrow.

Sacrifice and pride have been a consistent, engaging theme for me as a parent. Sacrifice is required even more when you are supporting multiple children in different houses. My particular dynamic is I have a child who is two counties away and a child who is two states away, which is a new limitation. There are times I have to go out of state to support Isaiah, which may impact a weekend I was supposed to spend with my eldest David Jon. The answer to these dilemmas is always communication and to include planning. Because I do not live in the same house as their mothers, their interest is in the child that we share, not the equal sharing of resources and time that I must give to all of my children. As the dad in this situation, like many other men, my goal is for my kids to be close to each other and know they are my priority. If I were to live in the house with their mother, the mom and I would split tasks or events to attend if our two kids had something to do at the same time. Offering the same coverage and consideration is not an option. Should everyone worry about themselves, or worry about all kids involved? For example, I have to make a decision if my son's birthday is the same week as the day my other son decides he wants to go to a sports camp. There was not any planning in regards to the son attending camp, and my resources can only support one occasion. My gut says, invest in the birthday because that is an annual celebration, but the mother of the son going to camp has no regard that it is the brother's birthday. If we all lived together, there would be a consideration for all kids. Children have to compete with their parents' schedule and their sibling events and needs all the time. Ideally, good parents should support, and have empathy for the totality of the situation. Arrangements become complicated as soon as the parents decide their relationship cannot continue. Expect barriers, but most importantly, protect the intentions, efforts, and integrity of the other parent should be a courtesy because there are no winners when you paint the other parent in a bad light. There are always two sides to shared custody.

I often find myself laying down my pride for my sons when it comes to interacting with irrational mother moments, or road rage. At times I do not give a response to false information presented or accusations made by my child's mother, to promote peace. Like I mentioned earlier in the book, I do not have to win every disagreement. I recently was moving to a new home with my wife who is expecting a baby, and we ended up with unexpected expenses for the purchase of necessary supplies, as well as the cost of moving the home, totaling over $5000, resulting in the depletion of my savings account. My eldest asks me to buy him some summer clothes, even though his mother could have used the bi-weekly financial support if that was a high concern. I tell her I will pitch in on my next check because I'm broke until then. His mother's response was, "This is very disappointing." Not realizing I just bought him some new luggage for his summer vacation in the same pay-period while moving. I think that merited a harsh response from me, but I said, "You are blind to other circumstances." Meaning, I have other expenses, which you do not know about. When parents are no longer in a relationship, situations like this often turn into opposition, which is not healthy, and it does not have to be that way! Even though I am not in a relationship with David Jon's mom, I still defend her, even when it's hard to do so. Why? That is my son's mom, and she is an extension of him, and if she is in despair or her reputation is being unfairly portrayed I have to step up because it can have an indirect impact and/or result in a complex for my son.

During my busy move, I had the pleasure of attending my son, David Jon's, elementary school graduation. The day of his graduation my pregnant wife and son Isaiah had to stay at a friend's house because our new place was not ready. There was nothing that was going to keep me from attending this special day. Not the 135-mile drive, the traffic, or the lack of sleep from the night before. I was proud of my son participating and receiving additional awards at the graduation. I also showed my gratitude towards his mom for the job well done that she is doing. If I added up the physical time he stayed with me year-round it would be around 25 percent of the time. His mom deserves more credit, period. It is always good to give credit when it is due and well deserved. There was a hidden blessing that day that had nothing to do with my son. During David Jon's elementary graduation, the school dedicated a portion of the ceremony to recognize the special-needs students who were being promoted to the next grade level. At that moment, watching kids who were in wheelchairs with special needs getting assistance to the platform to receive their diploma, and watching their family members' cheer, clap, and cry, I realized my sacrifice that day and that week was not comparable to what these special-needs-student providers are committed to contributing daily. I salute the parents who are always fighting to encourage and deliver hope and a smile to their kid's life. These children have medical challenges and lack the ability to do the simple things in life for themselves. Many parents remain in the fight after recognizing their kids will never be independent and these particular parents do not forsake their responsibility.

Many people are not built to be a qualified guardian, especially when there are special circumstances. But I am not in favor of condemning an adult who threw in the towel while trying to raise their child the right way. Sometimes it is in the child's best interest to go to the nearest relative.

I feel blessed to be a father, and I embrace the challenges that this title comes with, even if it comes down to beating and conquering my ideology and traditional beliefs. Fatherhood is the best hood, where men can use their hands and heart to build the best part of them. The best part of waking up is sharing breakfast time with my kids. Don't forfeit golden opportunities between parent and child due to ego or unwillingness to do what is best for the relationship. As the parent, we are ahead of the class and should be the managers of the relationship between child and parent. We know the issue that was present in our parental involvement and should be doing our best to avoid those pitfalls. As generations continue to grow, there will be new problems to address, and as parents let's not use archaic, ineffective tools to remedy these problems.

Parenting is not easy and has no room for a lazy adult who is not investing in their parenting skills or styles. Parenting is about patience, support, love, and sacrifice. Moving from father to daddy is like moving from the general manager to the coach. Many GM's are content with the title and prefer directing from a distance. The coach is in there every day

FROM FATHER TO DADDY

doing the day-to-day directing, which includes traveling with the players. This book is to guide and applaud the men who are having a positive impact on and presence in their child's life. Even though as a man or parent you feel you are doing well, there is always room for improvement. Earn the name and the perks that come with "Daddy." Trust me; your kids will not let you carry it for long if you are not living up to the privilege. I love competing in sports and performing on the piano, but if there is only one thing in life that I continue to develop and improve it will be my positive parenting skills and loving relationship with my children.

126

ACKNOWLEDGMENTS

First, I would like to acknowledge all fathers and parents who have taken on the responsibility to love and raise kids.

My kids, David Jonny, Isaiah (the cheetah), Dylan Joy, and Christian Alexander for inspiring me and teaching me how to be a better father. Every time I hear you guys say, "Daddy" I'm ready to respond to your needs. I love you all!

Thank you to my father Anthony W. White for being an example of pure love and sacrifice. Also, other male figures that impacted me as a man or father just by observation and interaction. Uncle Rodney, Uncle Charles, and William A. Benson. Pastor Benson, I met you at 18-years-old and you bestowed priceless knowledge on me that helped shape me into a man.

My mother, Dr. Judy White, without you this project would not have been released. Not only did you financially invest (along with Kristina) you instilled in me the ambition to reach for the impossible. I love and thank you for the many roles you play in my life.

Thank you to my wife, Shanae, for supporting me in putting the house on hold to focus on my writing.

Thank you to other family members and friends for your words of support and encouragement: Mom-Michelle, James, Malcom, and Sharde'.

My wonder editor, Vanessa Gonzales (the Night Owl), for not only polishing my writing but believing in my message. Thank you. Two projects down and many more to go...

ABOUT THE AUTHOR

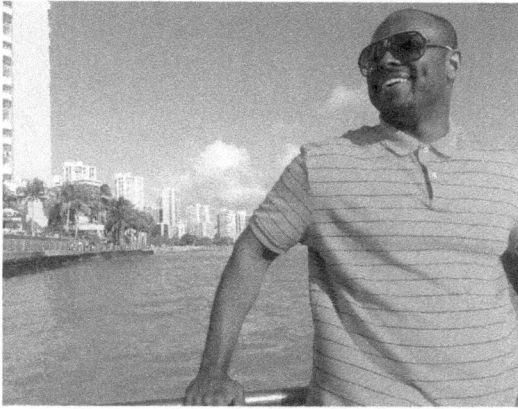

David A. White grew up in Highland, California. He has a Master of Arts in Organizational Leadership from Azusa Pacific University. By day, he is a Contract Specialist for the U.S. Navy, and by night, a musician and writer. His other publications include *Rushing to Fail,* a motivational book for young adults on transitioning to independence for the right reasons; as well as *Six Women 6 Flavors: From Your Head to Your Bed* penned under A.D. White. He currently resides in San Diego, California with his wife, and is the father of four children. Learn more and follow his work at DavidWhiteAuthor.com.

www.ingramcontent.com/pod-product-compliance
Lightning Source LLC
Chambersburg PA
CBHW031625040426
42452CB00007B/680